Keeping Home

BY KNIT PICKS

Photography by Amy Cave

Printed in the United States of America

First Printing, 2017

ISBN 978-1-62767-152-1

Versa Press, Inc
800-447-7829

www.versapress.com

CONTENTS

K = knit, C = crochet

Not Your Granny's Kitchen Set

Double crochet granny triangles make up these fun kitchen items, putting a more modern shape to an old classic. If you've crocheted granny squares you'll have no problem with granny triangles, but if this is your first time the pattern walks you through them. This little set will make a fantastic hostess gift if you can manage to give them away once you're finished!

Happy Crocheting!

Allyson Dykhuizen

HANGING DISH TOWEL

FINISHED MEASUREMENTS

13" wide at bottom, 13" long plus 5 ½" hanger

YARN

Knit Picks Dishie (100% Cotton: 190 yards/100g): Swan 25409 (C1), Begonia 25790 (C2), 1 ball each

HOOKS

US G-6 (4 mm) crochet hook or size to obtain gauge

NOTIONS

Yarn Needle
1" button

GAUGE

12 sts and 10 rows = 4" over double crochet

Hanging Dish Towel

Notes:

Granny Triangles

Rnd 1: Chain 4 and join to create a loop. Ch 3, this will serve as the last DC of the last granny cluster. *3 DC, ch 1; rep from * 1 time more, 2 DC, slip st into the 2nd ch of the original 3 ch to finish rnd.

Rnd 2: Ch 3, this will serve as the last DC of the last granny cluster. Work 3 DC into the space between the 2 granny clusters directly below your ch. Ch 1. *in the space between the next 2 granny clusters work a corner by working 3 DC, ch 1, 3 DC into this space, ch 1; rep from * 1 time more. Work 2 DC into space before original ch, slip st into the 2nd ch of the 3 ch to finish rnd.

Rnd 3: Ch 3, this will serve as the last DC of the last granny cluster. Work 3 DC into the space between the 2 granny clusters directly below your ch. Ch 1. *3 DC into the space between the next 2 granny clusters. Ch 1. Work corner by working 3 DC, ch 1, 3 DC into the space between the next 2 granny clusters. Ch 1; rep from * 1 time more. Work 3 DC into next space between granny clusters. Ch 1. Work 2 DC into space before original ch, slip st into the 2nd ch of the 3 ch to finish rnd.

Rnd 4: Ch 3. This will serve as the last DC of the last granny cluster. Work 3 DC into the space between the 3 granny clusters directly below your ch. Ch 1. *3 DC in the space between next 2 granny clusters, ch1, 3 DC in the next space between next 2 granny clusters, ch 1. Work corner by working 3 DC, ch 1, 3 DC into this space between the next 2 granny clusters. Ch 1; rep from * 1 time more. Work 3 DCs in the space between next 2 granny clusters, ch 1, 3 DC in space between next 2 granny clusters, ch 1, 2 DC into space before original ch, slip st into the 2nd ch of the 3 ch to finish rnd.

Continue in the manner, adding one 3 DC cluster to each side between corners each rnd.

DIRECTIONS

With C1 start Granny Triangles pattern. Work rnds 1 and 2 in C2, rnd 3 in C1, rnds 4 and 5 in C2, rnd 6 in MC, rnds 7 and 8 in C2, rnd 9 in C1, rnds 10 and 11 in C2.

Rnd 12: With C1 reattach yarn at space to the left of the center top corner. Ch 2, 2 DC into same space, continue around in pattern to last space before top corner. SC in each st of corner 5 sts to center of corner, 5 st to finish rnd – 10 sc. Ch 2, work 10 DC across previous 10 sc sts. Continue working 10 sts in DC until hanger measures 5 ½". Fasten off.

Finishing

Weave in ends. Sew button to RS center of sc row at base of hanger. Fasten by forcing button between 2 DC.

NOT YOUR GRANNY'S
DISHCLOTH

FINISHED MEASUREMENTS
12" diameter circle

YARN
Knit Picks Dishie (100% Cotton; 190 yards/100g): Begonia 25790 (C1), Swan 25409 (C2), Blush 26668 (C3), 1 ball each

HOOKS
US G-6 (4 mm) crochet hook or size to obtain gauge

NOTIONS
Yarn Needle

GAUGE
12 sts and 10 rows = 4" in double crochet

Dishcloth

Notes:

Granny Triangles

Rnd 1: Chain 4 and join to create a loop. Ch 3, this will serve as the last DC of the last granny cluster. *3 DC, ch 1; rep from * 1 time more, 2 DC, slip st into the 2nd ch of the original 3 ch to finish rnd.

Rnd 2: Ch 3, this will serve as the last DC of the last granny cluster. Work 3 DC into the space between the 2 granny clusters directly below your ch. Ch 1. *in the space between the next 2 granny clusters work a corner by working 3 DC, ch 1, 3 DC into this space, ch 1; rep from * 1 time more. Work 2 DC into space before original ch, slip st into the 2nd ch of the 3 ch to finish rnd.

Rnd 3: Ch 3, this will serve as the last DC of the last granny cluster. Work 3 DC into the space between the 2 granny clusters directly below your ch. Ch 1. *3 DC into the space between the next 2 granny clusters. Ch 1. Work corner by working 3 DC, ch 1, 3 DC into the space between the next 2 granny clusters. Ch 1; rep from * 1 time more. Work 3 DC into next space between granny clusters. Ch 1. Work 2 DC into space before original ch, slip st into the 2nd ch of the 3 ch to finish rnd.

Rnd 4: Ch 3. This will serve as the last DC of the last granny cluster. Work 3 DC into the space between the 3 granny clusters directly below your ch. Ch 1. *3 DC in the space between next 2 granny clusters, ch1, 3 DC in the next space between next 2 granny clusters, ch 1. Work corner by working 3 DC, ch 1, 3 DC into this space between the next 2 granny clusters. Ch 1; rep from * 1 time more. Work 3 DCs in the space between next 2 granny clusters, ch 1, 3 DC in space between next 2 granny clusters, ch 1, 2 DC into space before original ch, slip st into the 2nd ch of the 3 ch to finish rnd.

Continue in the manner, adding 1 3 DC cluster to each side between corners each rnd.

DIRECTIONS

Make four 6 rnd granny triangles.

1 – [2 rnds C1, 1 rnd C2] twice.

2 – [2 rnds C2, 1 rnd C1] twice.

3 – [2 rnds C3, 1 rnd C2] twice.

4 – [2 rnds C2, 1 rnd C3] twice.

Finishing

With tops of granny triangles to the center and wrong sides together, seam triangles together with SC crisscrossing lengths of circle. Weave in ends.

NOT YOUR GRANNY'S
MUG COZY

FINISHED MEASUREMENTS
10" long and 2" wide

YARN
Knit Picks Dishie (100% Cotton; 190
yards/100g): Begonia 25790 (C1), Swan
25409 (C2), Blush 26668 (C3), 1 ball each

HOOKS
US G-6 (4 mm) crochet hook, or size to
obtain gauge

NOTIONS
Yarn Needle
1" button

GAUGE
12 sts and 10 rows = 4" in double crochet

Mug Cozy

DIRECTIONS

With C3, ch 32.

DC in 3rd ch from hook and every ch to end.– 30 DCs.

DC 1 row in C2.

DC 1 row in C1.

DC 1 row in C2.

DC 1 row in C3.

With C2 attach yarn to end of C2 stripe and chain for 3", attach end to other C2 stripe to create a loop.

Finishing

Weave in ends. Attach button to RS C1 center stripe after measuring the cozy around your cup for fit.

Ombre Sea Kitchen Set

This pretty kitchen set is knit in a simple linen stitch, with a tranquil ombre striping added for a fun and updated look, as well as looking great on both sides of the projects. The hand towel is topped with a handy tab for a secure fit on your towel holder. The matching half-apron features a unique after-thought pocket that hides invisibly beneath the apron, revealing a fun little pop of color just at the top opening.

Happy Knitting!

Kalurah Hudson

OMBRE SEA
DISHCLOTH

FINISHED MEASUREMENTS
6.5" square, blocked

YARN
Knit Picks Comfy Worsted (75% Pima Cotton, 25% Acrylic; 109 yards/50g): MC White 25315, CC1 Celestial 25314, CC2 Light Blue 25311; 1 ball each

NEEDLES
US 9 (5.5mm) circular needles, or size to obtain gauge

NOTIONS
Yarn Needle

GAUGE
24 sts and 36 rows = 4" in Linen stitch, blocked

Dishcloth

Linen Stitch

Row 1: (WS) (Sl1 wyif, K1) rep to end.
Row 2: (Sl1 wyib, P1) rep to end.

For a tutorial on the **Long Tail Cast On**, please see
http://tutorials.knitpicks.com/wptutorials/long-tail-cast-on/

DIRECTIONS

CO 40 sts with MC using Long Tail Cast On..

Row 1: WS (Sl1 wyif, K1) rep to end.
Row 2: (Sl1 wyib, P1) rep to end.
Row 3: Rep row 1.
Row 4: With CC1, rep row 2.
Row 5: With CC1, rep row 1.
Row 6: With MC, rep row 2.
Row 7: With MC, rep row 1.
Row 8: With CC1, rep row 2.
Row 9: With CC1, rep row 1.
Row 10: With MC, rep row 2.
Row 11: With MC, rep row 1.
Row 12: With CC2, rep row 2.
Row 13: With CC2, rep row 1.
Row 14: With MC, rep row 2.
Row 15: With MC, rep row 1.
Row 16: With CC2, rep row 2.

Row 17: With CC2, rep row 1.
Row 18: With MC, rep row 2.
Row 19: With MC, rep row 1.
Row 20-37: Rep rows 18 & 19 for 18 rows.
Row 38: With CC2, rep row 2.
Row 39: With CC2, rep row 1.
Row 40: With MC, rep row 2.
Row 41: With MC, rep row 1.
Row 42: With CC2, rep row 2.
Row 43: With CC2, rep row 1.
Row 44: With MC, rep row 2.
Row 45: With MC, rep row 1.
Row 46: With CC1, rep row 2.
Row 47: With CC1, rep row 1.
Row 48: With MC, rep row 2.
Row 49: With MC, rep row 1.
Row 50: With CC1, rep row 2.
Row 51: With CC1, rep row 1.
Row 52: With MC, rep row 2.
Row 53: With MC, rep row 1.
Row 54-58: Rep row 52 & 53.

WS Bind off: (Using size US #6 dpn) Sl1wyif, K1, PSO, (sl1 wyif, PSO, K1, PSO) rep to end.

Break yarn and pull through rem st.

Finishing

Weave in ends and block if desired.

OMBRE SEA
HAND TOWEL

FINISHED MEASUREMENTS

6.5" wide x 14" long, with tab unbuttoned, blocked

YARN

Knit Picks Comfy Worsted (75% Pima Cotton, 25% Acrylic; 109 yards/50g): MC White 25315, CC1 Celestial 25314, CC2 Light Blue 25311; 1 ball each.

NEEDLES

US 9 (5.5mm) 9" Straight needles

NOTIONS

Yarn Needle
One .5" Button

GAUGE

24 sts and 36 rows = 4" in Linen stitch, blocked.

Hand Towel

Linen Stitch

Row 1: (WS) (Sl1 wyif, K1) rep to end.
Row 2: (Sl1 wyib, P1) rep to end.

For a tutorial on the **Long Tail Cast On**, please see
http://tutorials.knitpicks.com/wptutorials/long-tail-cast-on/

DIRECTIONS

CO 40 sts with MC, using Long Tail Cast On.
Row 1: WS (Sl1 wyif, K1) rep to end.
Row 2: (Sl1 wyib, P1) rep to end.
Row 3: Rep row 1.
Row 4: With CC1, rep row 2.
Row 5: With CC1, rep row 1.
Row 6: With MC, rep row 2.
Row 7: With MC, rep row 1.
Row 8: With CC1, rep row 2.
Row 9: With CC1, rep row 1.
Row 10: With MC, rep row 2.
Row 11: With MC, rep row 1.
Row 12: With CC2, rep row 2.
Row 13: With CC2, rep row 1.
Row 14: With MC, rep row 2.
Row 15: With MC, rep row 1.
Row 16: With CC2, rep row 2.
Row 17: With CC2, rep row 1. Cut CC2 yarn, leaving a 6" tail for

weaving in. MC is used for the rest of hand towel.
Row 18: With MC, rep row 2.
Row 19: With MC, rep row 1.
Row 20-89: Rep rows 18 & 19 for 18 rows.
Row 90: Decrease – (Sl1 wyib, P3tog) rep to end. (20sts)
Row 91: (Sl1 wyif, K1) rep to end.
Row 92: Decrease – Rep row 90. (10sts)
Row 93-119: Tab – Rep rows 1 & 2 for 27 rows.
Row 120: Button hole – (Sl1 wyib, P1) twice, sl1 wyib, YO twice, (P1, sl1 wyib) twice, P1. (12sts)
Row 121: Decrease – (Sl1 wyif, K1) twice, sl2 wyif, YIB, K2tog, (sl1 wyif, K1) twice. (11sts)
Row 122: Decrease - (Sl1 wyib, P1) twice, sl1 wyib, P2tog, (sl1 wyib, P1) twice. (10sts)
WS Bind off: (Using size US #6 dpn) Sl1 wyif, K1, PSO, (sl1 wyif, PSO, K1, PSO) rep to end. Break yarn and pull through rem st.

Finishing

Sew button onto the bottom end of the tab. Fold the tab down WS facing, to determine where the button should be sewn on. Weave in ends.

OMBRE SEA
APRON

FINISHED MEASUREMENTS

Apron: 18" wide x 15" long; Pocket: 6" deep x
9" wide (at opening), 10" wide (at fold); Belt:
95" long, end to end, blocked

YARN

Knit Picks Comfy Worsted (75% Pima
Cotton, 25% Acrylic; 109 yards/50g):
MC White 25315, 2 skeins ; CC1 Celestial
25314, CC2 Light Blue 25311; 1 ball each.

NEEDLES

US 6 (4mm) DPN for binding off
US 9 (5.5mm) 9" Straight needles, 16"
circular needles and 40" circular needles, or
size to obtain gauge

NOTIONS

Yarn Needle
Waste yarn
Spare needle OR stitch holder (to hold 100
sts)

GAUGE

24 sts and 36 rows = 4" in Linen stitch,
blocked, with size 9 needles.

Apron

Linen Stitch
Row 1: (WS) (Sl1 wyif, K1) rep to end.
Row 2: (Sl1 wyib, P1) rep to end.

Kitchener Stitch
Hold the two pieces of knitting parallel to one another with the wrong sides facing. Thread the working yarn with a yarn needle. *Insert the yarn needle knitwise into the first stitch on the front knitting needle. Draw through the stitch and slip the stitch off of the front needle. Insert the yarn needle purlwise into the next stitch on the front knitting needle. Draw through the stitch. Leave the stitch on the needle. Insert the yarn needle purlwise into the first stitch on the back knitting needle. Draw through the stitch and slip the stitch off of the back needle. Insert the yarn needle knitwise into the next stitch on the back knitting needle. Draw through the stitch. Leave the stitch on the needle. Repeat these steps beginning at the * until all of your stitches have been grafted together.

For a tutorial on the **Long Tail Cast On**, please see http://tutorials.knitpicks.com/wptutorials/long-tail-cast-on/

For a tutorial on the purled cast on, please see http://www.stitchdiva.com/tutorials/knitting/knit-on-purl-on

DIRECTIONS
Using Size 9 40" circular, CO 100 sts with MC using Long Tail Cast On.

Row 1: WS (Sl1 wyif, K1) rep to end.
Row 2: (Sl1 wyib, P1) rep to end.
Row 3: Rep row 1.
Row 4: With CC1, rep row 2.
Row 5: With CC1, rep row 1.
Row 6: With MC, rep row 2.
Row 7: With MC, rep row 1.
Row 8: With CC1, rep row 2.
Row 9: With CC1, rep row 1.
Row 10: With MC, rep row 2.
Row 11: With MC, rep row 1.
Row 12: With CC2, rep row 2.
Row 13: With CC2, rep row 1.

Row 14: With MC, rep row 2.
Row 15: With MC, rep row 1.
Row 16: With CC2, rep row 2.
Row 17: With CC2, rep row 1. Cut CC2 yarn, leaving a 6" tail for weaving in. MC is used for the rest of hand twoel.

Row 18: With MC, rep row 2.
Row 19: With MC, rep row 1.
Row 20-111: Rep rows 18 & 19 for 91 rows. Or approx. 13" from CO edge.

Row 112: Insert Pocket – Still using MC, (Sl1 wyib, P1) 15 times, drop working yarn, K40 sts with waste yarn, place these 40 sts back onto the LHN, knit these 40 sts agian using working yarn, (Sl1wyib, P1) 15x.

Row 113-123: Rep rows 18 & 19 for 11 rows. Place all stitches onto a spare needle or stitch holder that can be knitted off of.

Row 124: Belt – With CC1 and empty circular needle, CO 200 sts, using purled cast on, (Sl1 wyib, P1) 50x over sts in spare needle, CO another 200 sts using purled cast on. (500 sts)

Row 125-130: Using CC1, rep rows 1 & 2 for 6 rows.

WS Bind off: (Using size US #6 dpn) Sl1 wyif, (K1, PSO) rep to end. Break yarn and pull through rem st.

Invisible Pocket
Using size Size 9 16" circular:
From WS of apron, remove waste sts and place all 40 live sts onto circular needle. Now flip the needle to the RS of the apron.

Using CC2, knit in the round until pocket measures 6". Break yarn, leaving a tail about 6x the width of the pocket. Distribute sts evenly onto two separate needles. Weave tail through yarn needle. With knit sts facing you, work Kitchener's Stitch to join both sides of the pocket together. Turn pocket inside out so purl stitches are on the outside. Tuck inside of apron.

Finishing
Weave in all ends. Lightly steam press the pocket with a damp rag and iron set to low heat, to make pocket lie down flat (if needed).

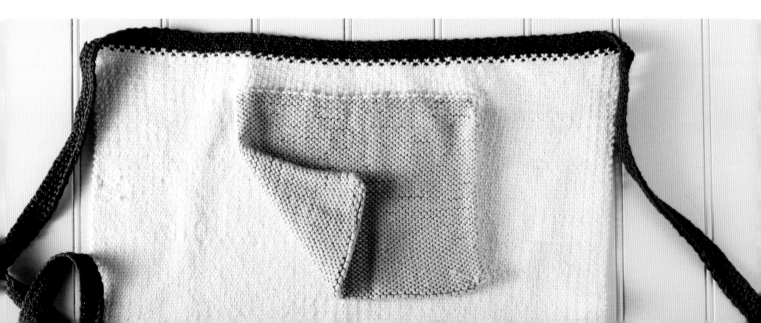

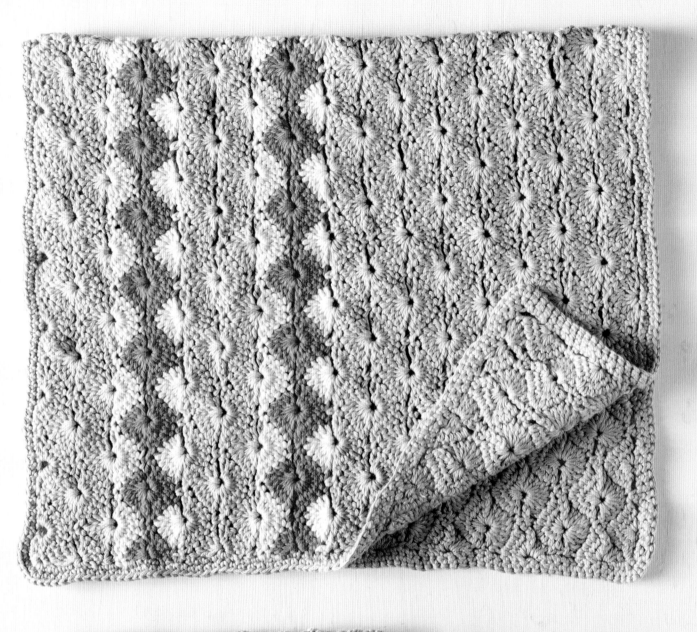

Morning Sunburst Kitchen Set

Create a classy retro look in your kitchen with this easy
to create set featuring the Catherine Wheel or Starburst
stitch. This stitch pattern creates beautiful lines and
intriguing textures within the fabric of your work.

Happy Crocheting!

Beth Major

FINISHED MEASUREMENTS

9.5" square, approximately

YARN

Knit Picks Shine Sport (60% Pima Cotton, 40% Modal®; 110 yards/50g): MC Platinum 25338, C1 Cream 23615, C2 Grapefruit 25778, 1 ball each

HOOKS

Hook G/6, 4.00mm

NOTIONS

Yarn Needle

GAUGE

16 sts and 8 rows = 4" in DC, lightly blocked

Dishcloth

Notes:

Special Stitches

4 Double Crochet together (4Dctog)

(YO, insert hook in next st, Yo and pull up a loop, YO and pull through 2 loops, leave remaining loops on hook) 4 times, YO and pull through all 5 loops.

9 Double Crochet together (9DCtog)

YO, insert hook in next st, Yo and pull up a loop, YO and pull through 2 loops, leave remaining loops on hook) 9 times, YO and pull through all 10 loops.

DIRECTIONS

Row 1: With MC, CH 42, SC in 2nd CH from hook, (sk next 3 CH, 9 DC in next CH, sk next 3 CH, SC in next CH) repeat across.

Row 2: CH 4, turn, 4DCtog over next 4 sts, CH 4, SC in next st, CH 4, (9DCtog over next 9 sts, CH 4, SC in next st, CH 4) repeat across to last 5 sts, 5 DCtog over last 5 sts.

Row 3: CH 3, turn, 4 DC in 1st st (center of grouping), sk next 4 CH, SC in next SC, sk next 4 CH, (9 DC in centre of next grouping, sk next 4 CH, SC in next SC, sk next 4 CH) repeat across to last st, 5 DC in last st.

Row 4: CH 1, turn, SC in 1st st, CH 4, 9 DCtog over next 9 sts, CH 4, (SC in next st, CH 4, 9 DCtog over next 9 sts, CH 4) repeat across, SC in last st.

Row 5: Switch to color C1, CH 1, turn, SC in 1st st, (sk next 4 CH, 9 DC in center of next grouping, sk next 4 CH, SC in next st).

Rows 6-7: Switch to color C2, repeat rows 2 and 3.

Row 8: Switch to C1, repeat row 4.

Row 9: Switch to MC, repeat row 5.

Rows 10-18: Continuing in color MC, repeat rows 2-5 twice, repeat row 2 once, CH 1..

Finishing

Rnd 1: Continuing in color MC, 3 SC in same st, (evenly space 40 SC along edge, 3 SC in corner st) repeat 3 times, evenly space 40 SC along last edge, join last st to first st with a SL ST.

Rnd 2: CH 1, SC in same st, 3 SC in next SC, (SC in each SC down edge, 3 SC in corner) repeat 3 times, SC in each SC along last edge, join last st to first st with a SL ST, CH 1. Fasten off and weave in ends.

MORNING SUNBURST
HAND TOWEL

FINISHED MEASUREMENTS
Approximately 16.5" by 27.5"

YARN
Knit Picks Shine Sport (60% Pima Cotton, 40% Modal®; 110 yards/50g): MC Platinum 25338, 3 balls; C1 Cream 23615, C2 Grapefruit 25778, 1 ball each

HOOKS
Hook G/6, 4.00mm

NOTIONS
Yarn Needle

GAUGE
16 sts and 8 rows = 4" in DC, lightly blocked

Hand Towel

Notes:

Special Stitches

4 Double Crochet together (4Dc tog)
(YO, insert hook in next st, Yo and pull up a loop, YO and pull through 2 loops, leave remaining loops on hook) 4 times, YO and pull through all 5 loops.

9 Double Crochet together (9DCtog)
(YO, insert hook in next st, Yo and pull up a loop, YO and pull through 2 loops, leave remaining loops on hook) 9 times, YO and pull through all 10 loops.

DIRECTIONS

Row 1: With color MC, CH 122, SC in 2nd CH from hook, (sk next 3 CH, 9 DC in next CH, sk next 3 CH, SC in next CH) repeat across.

Row 2: CH 4, turn, 4DCtog over next 4 sts, CH 4, SC in next st, CH 4, (9DCtog over next 9 sts, CH 4, SC in next st, CH 4) repeat across to last 5 sts, 5 DCtog over last 5 sts.

Row 3: CH 3, turn, 4 DC in 1st st (centre of grouping), sk next 4 CH, SC in next SC, sk next 4 CH, (9 DC in center of next grouping, sk next 4 CH, SC in next SC, sk next 4 CH) repeat across to last st, 5 DC in last st.

Row 4: CH 1, turn, SC in 1st st, CH 4, 9 DCtog over next 9 sts, CH 4, (SC in next st, CH 4, 9 DCtog over next 9 sts, CH 4) repeat across, SC in last st.

Row 5: Switch to color C1, CH 1, turn, SC in 1st st, (sk next 4 CH,9 DC in center of next grouping, sk next 4 CH, SC in next st).

Rows 6-7: Switch to color C2, repeat rows 2 and 3.

Row 8: Switch to color C1, repeat row 4.

Rows 9-12: Switch to color MC, repeat row 5 then repeat rows 2-4

Rows 13-16: Switch to color C1, repeat row 5 then repeat rows 6-8, using C2 for rows 6 and 7 and C1 for row 8.

Rows 17: Switch to color MC, repeat row 5.

Rows 18-32: Continuing in color MC, repeat rows 2-5 three more times, repeat rows 2-4 once more, CH 1.

Finishing

Rnd 1: Continuing in color MC, 3 SC in same st, *evenly space 72 SC along edge, 3 SC in corner st, work 120 SC along next edge,* 3 SC in corner, repeat from * to * once, join last st to first st with a SL ST.

Rnd 2: CH 1, SC in same st, 3 SC in next SC, (SC in each SC down edge, 3 SC in corner) repeat 3 times, SC in each SC along last edge, join last st to first st with a SL ST, CH 1. Fasten off and weave in ends.

MORNING SUNBURST
CUP COZY

FINISHED MEASUREMENTS
Approximately 3" by 9.5"

YARN
Knit Picks Shine Sport (60% Pima Cotton, 40% Modal®); 110 yards/50g): MC Platinum 25338, C1 Cream 23615, C2 Grapefruit 25778, 1 ball each

HOOKS
Hook G/6, 4.00mm

NOTIONS
Yarn Needle

GAUGE
16 sts and 8 rows = 4" in DC, lightly blocked

Cup Cozy

Notes:

Special Stitches

4 Double Crochet together (4Dctog)

YO, insert hook in next st, Yo and pull up a loop, YO and pull through 2 loops, leave remaining loops on hook) 4 times, YO and pull through all 5 loops.

9 Double Crochet together (9DCtog)

(YO, insert hook in next st, Yo and pull up a loop, YO and pull through 2 loops, leave remaining loops on hook) 9 times, YO and pull through all 10 loops.

Foundation Single Crochet (FSC): CH 2, insert hook into first CH, YO and pull up loop, YO and pull through one loop (CH 1 made), YO and pull through both loops (SC made). *Insert hook into CH just made, YO and pull up a loop, YO and pull through one loop (CH 1 made), YO and pull through both loops (SC made)* Repeat from * to* as many times as required.

DIRECTIONS

Row 1: With color MC, FSC 33.

Row 2: CH 1, turn, SC in 1st st, (sk next 3 sts, 9 DC in next st, sk next 3sts, SC in next st) repeat across.

Row 3: Switch to color C1, CH 2, turn, HDC in 1st st and in each st across.

Row 4: Switch to color C2, CH 4, turn, 4DCtog over next 4 sts, CH 4, SC in next st, CH 4, (9DCtog over next 9 sts, CH 4, SC in next st, CH 4) repeat across to last 5 sts, 5 DCtog over last 5 sts

Row 5: CH 3, turn, 4 DC in 1st st (center of grouping), sk next 4 CH, SC in next SC, sk next 4 CH, (9 DC in center of next grouping, sk next 4 CH, SC in next SC, sk next 4 CH) repeat across to last st, 5 DC in last st.

Row 6: Switch to color C1, CH 2, turn, HDC in 1st st and in each st across.

Row 7: Switch to color MC, CH 1, turn, CH 4, 9 DCtog over next 9 sts, CH 4, (SC in next st, CH 4, 9 DCtog over next 9 sts, CH 4) repeat across, SC in last st.

Finishing

Rnd 1: Continuing in color MC, CH 1, do not turn, 3 SC in same st, evenly space 13 SC down side of cozy, CH 1, turn, SC in first st and each st up side, 3SC in corner, Work 32 SC across row, 3 CH in corner, evenly space 13 SC down side, CH 1, turn, SC in first st and each st up side.

Rnd 2: CH 5, curl cozy so both short edges lie along side each other, join into corner of other edge with a SC, SC in each st down edge to corner, CH 5, join into corner of edge with a SC, SC back up to first CH.

Rnd 3: SC in each CH and SC a rnd handle opening to last st. Sl st in first st, fasten off and weave in ends.

Bit of Whimsy Bath Set

A Bit Of Whimsy Bath Set is a fun knit, made to transform your bathroom into a sweet sancutary. These 3 pieces will show off your knitting skills - practice intarsia with the washcloth, try out the loop stitch on the bath mitt and perfect the bubble stitch with the hand towel. Using the silky soft Shine Sport, this set is wonderful to pamper yourself with, or to give as a thoughtful gift.

Happy Knitting!

Emily Ringelman

BIT OF WHIMSY
WASHCLOTH

FINISHED MEASUREMENTS

10" Square

YARN

Knit Picks Shine Sport (60% Pima Cotton, 40% Modal®; 110 yards/50g): MC Pistachio 25779, CC White 24486, 1 ball each

NEEDLES

US 5 (3.75mm) straight or circular needles, or size to obtain gauge

NOTIONS

Yarn Needle
Stitch Markers

GAUGE

24 sts and 32 rows = 4" over St st worked flat, blocked

Washcloth

Notes:

This washcloth has garter stitch borders to prevent rolling, and it very helpfully reminds you to "wash" in intarsia!

DIRECTIONS

With MC and straight or circular needles, CO 60. K 7 rows.

Next Row (RS): K6, PM, join CC and begin working from Washcloth Chart, PM, end k6 with MC.

Next Row (WS): K6, sm, work Row 2 of Washcloth Chart, sm, K6. Work as established, remembering to read RS (odd rows) of Washcloth Chart from right to left and WS rows (even rows) of Washcloth Chart from left to right, slipping markers as you come to them, knitting the first and last 6 sts of every row.

When chart is complete, break CC and, using MC only, work for 5" as follows:

Row 1 (RS): K.
Row 2 (WS): K6, P48, K6.

Piece should measure 9" tall.

K 7 rows, then BO knitwise.

Finishing

Weave in ends, wash and block to diagram.

Washcloth Chart

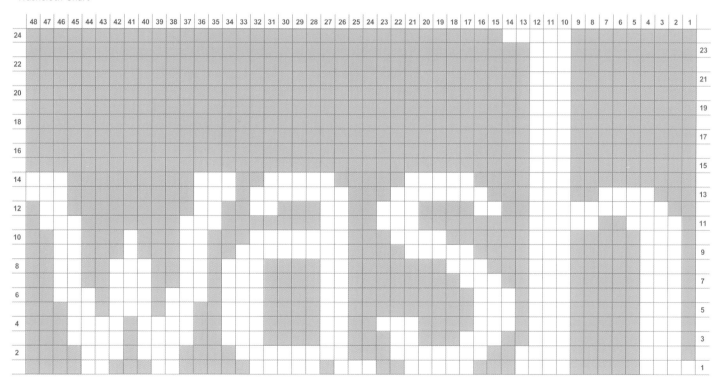

Legend

□ knit
RS: knit stitch
WS: purl stitch

▨ MC

□ CC

BIT OF WHIMSY
HAND TOWEL

FINISHED MEASUREMENTS
12" wide x 24" long

YARN
Knit Picks Shine Sport (60% Pima Cotton, 40% Modal®; 110 yards/50g): MC Pistachio 25779, 3 balls; CC1 White 24486 1 ball, CC2 Cosmopolitan 25344, 1 ball

NEEDLES
US 5 (3.75mm) straight or circular needles, or size to obtain gauge

NOTIONS
Yarn Needle
Stitch Markers

GAUGE
24 sts and 32 rows = 4" over St st worked flat, blocked

Hand Towel

Notes:

This hand towel has a fun and colorful dot pattern border on the two short edges. The edges of the towel are garter stitch to prevent rolling.

Bubble Stitch Pattern (worked flat beginning on the WS)

Row 1 (WS): With MC, P1, *P1 wrapping yarn twice around needle, P2, P1 wrapping yarn twice around needle, P1* to end.

Row 2 (RS): With CC, K1, sl 1 dropping extra loop, K2, sl 1 dropping extra loop, *[K1, yo, K1, yo, K1] into next st, sl 1 dropping extra loop, K2, sl 1 dropping extra loop* to last st, K1.

Row 3: With CC, P1, sl 1, P2, sl 1, *P5, sl 1, P2, sl 1* to last st, P1.

Row 4: With CC, K1, sl 1, K2, sl 1 *K5, sl 1, K2, sl 1* to last st, K1.

Row 5: With CC, P1, sl 1, P2, sl 1, *P3tog, P2tog, pass P3tog st over P2tog st, sl 1, P2, sl 1* to last st, P1.

Row 6: With MC, K1, *drop 1st slipped st from needle, sl 2, drop 2nd slipped st, with left needle pick up 1st dropped st, sl 2 back to left needle, pick up 2nd dropped st, K5* to end.

Row 7: With MC, P.

Row 8: With MC, K.

DIRECTIONS

With MC and straight or circular needles, CO 71 sts. K 5 rows. Join CC1 and work rows 1-8 of Bubble Pattern (see Stitches), then break CC1, join CC2, and work rows 1-8 of Bubble Pattern again. Break CC2, rejoin CC1, and work rows 1-7 once more.

Next Row (RS): K6, PM, K 59, PM, K6.

Next Row: K6, sm, P to m, sm, K6.

Continue as established, knitting the first and last 6 sts of each row, until piece measures 20" from cast on edge.

Join CC1 and work rows 1-8 of Bubble Pattern (see Stitches), then break CC1, join CC2, and work rows 1-8 of Bubble Pattern again.

Break CC2, rejoin CC1, and work rows 1-7 once more.

K 5 rows.
BO knitwise.

Finishing

Weave in ends, wash and block to diagram.

BIT OF WHIMSY
WASHING MITT

FINISHED MEASUREMENTS

Washing Mitt: 8 (9)" tall x 5.25 (5.75)" wide at widest point

YARN

Knit Picks Shine Sport (60% Pima Cotton, 40% Modal®; 110 yards/50g): MC Pistachio 25779, CC White 24486, 1 ball each

NEEDLES

US 5 (3.75mm) straight or circular needles, or size to obtain gauge

US 5 (3.75mm) DPNs or two 24" circular needles for two circulars technique, or one 32" or longer circular needle for Magic Loop technique, or size to obtain gauge

NOTIONS

Yarn Needle
Stitch Markers

GAUGE

Mitt: 24 sts and 32 rows = 4" over St st in the round, blocked

Washing Mitt

Notes:

This washing mitt is basically a big thumb-less mitten with a loop stitch pad sewn onto the hand. The loop stitch will help you get that soap nice and sudsy in the shower. Use it in lieu of a sponge or loofah to wash your kids, your dog, your car, or just yourself.

Twisted Rib (worked in the round)
Rnd 1: *K1tbl, P1* to end.
Repeat Rnd 1 for Twisted Rib.

Loop Stitch Pattern (worked flat)
Make Loop (ML): K1 leaving st on left needle, yarn forward, place your left thumb up against the knitting and wrap the yarn around thumb twice, insert tip of right needle under loops on thumb, from right to left, and K stitch again, sl st off left needle, yo, pass the two stitches just worked over the yo.
Row 1: K
Row 2: *K1, ML* to last 2 sts, K2.
Row 3: K
Row 4: K2, *ML, K1* to end.

DIRECTIONS

Mitt
With MC and needles for small diameter knitting in the round, CO 34 (40). Join to work in the round, being careful not to twist. PM for beginning of round.

Work in Twisted Rib (see stitches) for 2 (2.5)".

K 1 round.

Next Rnd: K17 (20), PM, K to end.

Increase Rnd: K1, M1R, K to 1 st before m, M1L, K1, sm, K1, M1R, K to 1 st before end of rnd, M1L, K1. 4 sts inc'd.
K 2 rounds.

Repeat the last 3 rnds 6 more times- 62 (68) sts.

K 8 (12) rnds.

Decrease Rnd: K1, SSK, K to 3 sts before M, K2tog, K1, sm, K1, SSK, K to 3 sts before end, K2tog, K1. 4 sts dec'd.
K 2 rounds.

Repeat the last 3 rounds 6 more times- 34 (40) sts.
Place the first 17 (20) sts onto one needle and the last 17 (20) sts onto another needle, with needle tips pointing to the right. Break yarn, leaving a good working length, and use the Kitchener stitch to graft the sides together.

Loop Stitch Pad
With CC and straight or circular needles, CO 12 (15) sts.
Work rows 1 & 2 of Loop Stitch Pattern (see Stitches).

Next Row (Row 3 of Loop Stitch Pattern): KFB, K to last st, KFB
Work 2 rows of Loop Stitch Pattern.

Repeat the last 3 rows four times more, working new increases into pattern as best you can; small amounts of fudging will be unnoticeable in the loop pattern. 22 (25) sts.

Work 3 rows as established.

Decrease Row: SSK, work in pattern to last 2 sts, K2tog.
Work 2 rows of Loop Stitch Pattern.

Repeat the last 3 rows four times more. 12 (15) sts remain.
BO loosely.

Finishing
Weave in ends, wash and block to diagram.
With CC, sew loop stitch pad to washing mitt, matching curved increase and decrease edges, centering pad on mitt.

Kawaii Spring Spa Set

This adorable spa set is the perfect project for bridesmaids' gifts, a shower present or just for you.

The set includes enough yarn to make 2 washcloths, 2 headbands and 8 small face tawashis, great for applying toner, removing makeup or scrubbing your face.

Featuring pretty puff stitches and a whimsical picot trim, you can easily mix and match the colorways for multiple gifts from just 3 balls of yarn.

Happy Crocheting!

Kalurah Hudson

KAWAII SPRING
WASHCLOTH

FINISHED MEASUREMENTS
5.5" Square, blocked

YARN
Knit Picks Comfy Worsted (75% Pima Cotton, 25% Acrylic; 109 yards/50g): (CC) White 25315, (MC1) Seafoam 24153, (MC2) Semolina 26979, 1 ball each

HOOK
US D (3.25mm) crochet hook, or size to obtain gauge

NOTIONS
Yarn Needle

GAUGE
24 sc and 24 rows = 4"

Washclcloth

Special Stitches

Picot

Ch 3, sl st in 1st ch to close. (1 picot complete)

Puff Stitch

(Yarn over hook, insert hook into stitch and pull up a loop) 4 times, (9 loops on hook) yarn over hook and pull through all loops on hook.

DIRECTIONS

Worked in rows. Picot border is worked in one round.

Using MC1 or MC2, loosely ch 26.

Row 1 (WS): DC in 6th ch from hook, [ch 1, sk next ch, DC in next ch] 10 times.

Row 2 (RS): Ch 4, turn, sk next ch-1 and dc, (puff stitch, ch 1, puff stitch) into next ch-1 sp, [ch 1, sk next ch-1 sp, DC in next dc, ch 1, DC in next dc, ch 1, sk next ch-1 sp and dc, (puff stitch, ch 1, puff stitch) into next ch-1 sp] twice, ch 1, DC in 3rd ch of TCH.

Row 3: Ch 4, turn, sk 1st ch, DC in 1st puff stitch, ch 1, DC in next puff stitch, [ch 1, DC in next dc, ch 1, sk next ch, DC in next dc, ch 1, sk next ch, DC in next puff stitch, ch 1, DC in next puff stitch] twice, ch 1, DC in 3rd ch of TCH.

Row 4: Ch 4, turn, sk 1st ch, DC in next dc, ch 1, sk next ch, DC in next dc, [ch 1, sk next ch-1 sp and dc, (puff stich, ch 1, puff stitch) into next ch-1 sp, ch 1, sk next dc and ch-1 sp, DC in next dc, ch 1,

sk next ch-1, DC in next dc] twice, ch 1, DC in 3rd ch of TCH.

Row 5: Rep row 3.

Row 6: Rep row 2.

Row 7: Rep row 3.

Row 8: Rep row 4.

Row 9: Rep row 3.

Row 10: Rep row 2.

Row 11: Rep row 3, finishing the last stitch of the row with CC yarn.

Row 12 (Picot Round): Using CC yarn, ch 1, turn, 2 SC into first ch-1 sp, sk next dc, (1 SC, picot, 1 SC) into next ch-1 sp, [sk next dc, 2 SC into next ch-1 sp, sk next dc, (1 SC, picot, 1 SC) into next ch-1 sp] 4 times, sk last dc, (2 SC, picot, 2 SC) into ch-4 sp, rotate cloth 90 degrees to the right, (1 SC, picot, 1 SC) into dc, [2 SC into ch-4 sp, (1 SC, picot, 1 SC into dc] 4 times, (2 SC, picot, 2 SC) into ch-5, rotate cloth 90 degrees to the right, (1 SC, picot, 1 SC) into next ch-1 sp, [2 SC into next ch-1 sp, (1 SC, picot, 1 SC) into next ch-1 sp)] 4 times, (2 SC, picot, 2 SC) into last ch-1 sp, rotate cloth 90 degrees to the right, (1 SC, picot, 1 SC) into first dc, (1 SC, picot, 1 SC) into next ch-4 sp, [2 SC into next dc, (1 SC, picot, 1 SC) into next ch-4 sp] 4 times, 2 SC into last dc, picot, sl st to 1st sc of row to join.

Finishing

Tie off. Weave in ends and block to finished dimensions, if desired.

Washcloth Chart

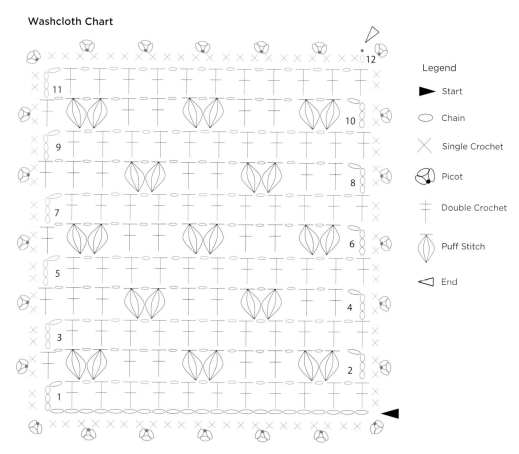

Legend

▶ Start

⬭ Chain

✕ Single Crochet

Picot

╪ Double Crochet

Puff Stitch

◁ End

Read all odd numbered rows from left to right
Read all even numbered rows from right to left

Red rows - wrong side of work
Black rows - right side of work
Green round - border (right side of work)

KAWAII SPRING
HEADBAND

FINISHED MEASUREMENTS

2.5" wide x 18.5" long, before assembling.
Finished circumference is 18", blocked

YARN

Knit Picks Comfy Worsted (75% Pima
Cotton, 25% Acrylic; 109 yards/50g):
(CC) White 25315, (MC1) Seafoam 24153,
(MC2) Semolina 26979, 1 ball each.

HOOK

US D (3.25mm) crochet hook, or size to
obtain gauge

NOTIONS

Yarn Needle
Elastic Ponytail Holder

GAUGE

24 sc and 24 rows = 4"

Headband

Special Stitches
Picot
Ch 3, sl st in 1st ch to close. (1 picot complete)

Puff Stitch
(Yarn over hook, insert hook into stitch and pull up a loop) 4 times, (9 loops on hook) yarn over hook and pull through all loops on hook.

DIRECTIONS

Worked in rows in MC1 or MC2. Picot border is worked in one round using CC. The tabs are worked last using the CC and sewn down over an elastic ponytail holder.

Using MC1 or MC2, loosely ch 14.
Row 1 (WS): DC in 6th ch from hook, [(ch 1, sk next ch 1, DC in next ch] 4 times.
Row 2: Ch 4, turn, sk 1st ch, DC in next dc, [ch 1, sk next ch-1 sp, DC in next dc] 3 times, ch 1, DC in 3rd ch of TCH.
Row 3: Rep row 2.
Row 4: Ch 4, turn, DC in next dc, ch 1, sk next ch-1 sp and dc, (puff stich, ch 1, puff stitch) into next ch-1 sp, ch 1, sk next dc and ch-1 sp, DC in next dc, ch 1, DC in 3rd ch of TCH.
Rows 5: Ch 4, turn, DC in 1st dc, ch 1, sk next ch-1 sp, DC in next puff stich, ch 1, sk next ch-1 sp, DC in next puff stitch, ch 1, sk next ch-1 sp, DC in next dc, ch 1, DC in 3rd ch of TCH.
Rows 6-7: Repeat row 2.
Rows 8-31: Repeat rows 4-7, six times, finishing off last stitch of row 31 with the CC yarn.

Row 32 (RS) (Picot Round): Using CC yarn, ch 1, turn, 2 SC into first ch-1 sp, 1 SC in next dc, [1 SC into next ch-1 sp, 1 SC into next dc] 3 times, (2 SC, picot, 2 SC) into ch-4 sp, rotate headband 90 degrees to the right, (1 SC, picot, 1 SC) into first dc, [2 SC into next ch-4 sp, (1 SC, picot, 1 SC) into next dc] 14 times, (2 SC, picot, 2 SC) into ch-5 sp, rotate headband 90 degrees to the right, 1 SC in bottom of 1st dc, [1 SC into next ch-1 sp, 1 SC in bottom of next dc] 3 times, (2 SC, picot, 2 SC) into last ch-1 sp, rotate headband 90 degrees to the right, (1 SC, picot, 1 SC) into next ch-4 sp, [2 SC into next dc, (1 SC, picot, 1 SC) into next ch-4 sp] 14 times, 2 SC into last dc, picot, sl st to 1st sc. Tie off.

Make Tabs for Headband

Join CC yarn to the headband, see chart for placement.

Row 1 (WS): Ch 1, do NOT turn, 1 SC in same st that you joined to, 1 SC in next 4 sc. (5scs)
Row 2: Ch 1, turn, 1 SC in each sc of row. (5scs)
Rows 3-7: Rep row 2.
Tie off, leaving an 8" tail for sewing down tab. Rep tab on other side of headband, also leaving a tail for sewing down tab.

Finishing

Sew one tab down over the ponytail holder (sandwiching the ponytail holder). Stitch the end of the tab down to the wrong side of the headband (where you joined the yarn to make the tab). Repeat this on the other tab, sandwiching the other side of the ponytail holder. This will join the headband to the ponytail holder and will create a nice, elastic back to the headband.
Weave in all ends and block to finished dimensions, if desired.

Headband Chart

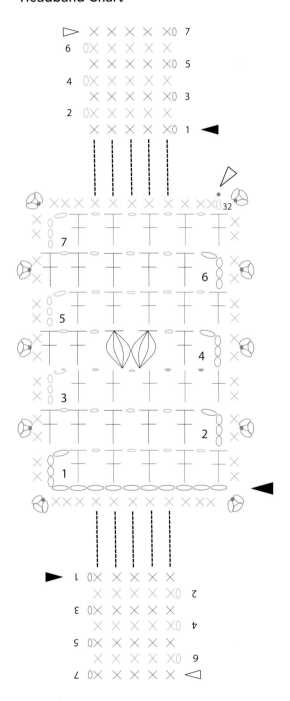

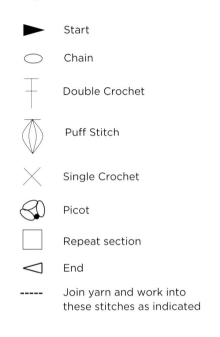

Legend

►   Start

◯   Chain

╤   Double Crochet

◈   Puff Stitch

✕   Single Crochet

❀   Picot

▢   Repeat section

◁   End

-----   Join yarn and work into these stitches as indicated

Red rows - wrong side of work
Black rows - right side of work
Green round - border (right side of work)

Read Red rows from left to right
Read Black rows from right to left
Read Green round from right to left

KAWAII SPRING
TAWASHI

FINISHED MEASUREMENTS
Tawashi: 3.25" across, blocked

YARN
Knit Picks Comfy Worsted (75% Pima
Cotton, 25% Acrylic; 109 yards/50g):
(CC) White 25315, (MC1) Seafoam 24153,
(MC2) Semolina 26979, 1 ball each.

HOOK
US D (3.25mm) crochet hook, or size to
obtain gauge

NOTIONS
Yarn Needle

GAUGE
24 sc and 24 rows = 4"

Tawashi

Special Stitches

Picot

Ch 3, sl st in 1st ch to close. (1 picot complete)

3 Half Double Crochet Decrease – 3HDCdec

(Yarn over hook, insert hook into stitch and pull up a loop) 3 times, (7 loops on hook) yarn over hook and pull through all loops on hook.

Puff Stitch

(Yarn over hook, insert hook into stitch and pull up a loop) 4 times, (9 loops on hook) yarn over hook and pull through all loops on hook.

DIRECTIONS

Worked in joined rounds. Picot round is worked in CC yarn.

Using MC1 or MC2, make a Magic Ring.

Rnd 1: Ch 3, do NOT turn, 1 3HDCdec into ring, [ch 2, puff stitch into ring] 5 times, ch 2, sl st to 3HDCdec, sl st in ch-2 sp.

Rnd 2: Ch 3, do NOT turn, (3HDCdec, ch 2, puff stitch) into ch-2 sp, ch 1, sk next puff stitch, [(puff stitch, ch 2, puff stitch) into next ch-2 sp, ch 1, sk next puff stitch] 4 times, (puff stitch, ch 2, puff stitch) into last ch-2 sp, ch 1, sl st to 3HDCdec, finishing off last st with CC yarn.

Rnd 3: Using CC yarn, ch 1, do NOT turn, 1 SC into same st previously slipped stitched into, 3 SC into ch-2 sp, 1 SC in next puff stitch, [(1 SC, picot, 1 SC) into next ch-1 sp, 1 SC in next puff stitch, 3 SC into next ch-2 sp, 1 SC in next puff stitch] 5 times, (1 SC, picot, 1 SC) into last ch-1 sp, sl st to 1st sc.

Tie off.

Finishing

Weave in all ends and block to finished dimensions, if desired.

Tawashi Chart

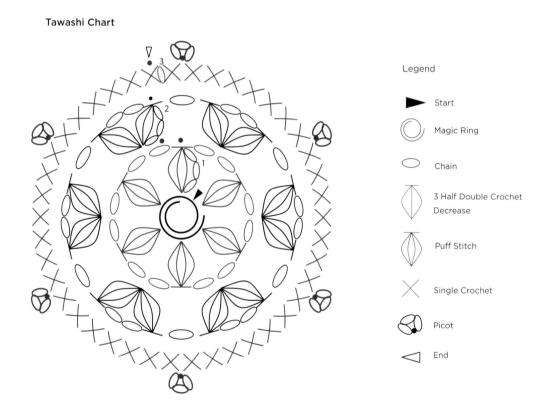

Work every round from right to left

Red - odd numbered round

Black - even numbered round

Legend

▶ Start

Magic Ring

Chain

3 Half Double Crochet Decrease

Puff Stitch

✕ Single Crochet

Picot

◁ End

Sand and Sea Bath Set

A trip to the beach is a fun adventure that usually includes searching the shore for beautiful shells. The Sand and Sea bath set includes three pieces shaped like some of the most interesting shells: a sea snail bath mat, a hand towel with sea stars, and a sea urchin washcloth. Worked in a cotton acrylic blend, the set is very absorbent and easily laundered, making it a perfect fit for the bathroom. With this set, it's easy to have a beach adventure in your own home!

Happy Knitting!

Joyce Fassbender

SAND AND SEA

SEA URCHIN WASHCLOTH

FINISHED MEASUREMENTS
10" diameter

YARN
Knit Picks Comfy Worsted (75% Pima Cotton, 25% Acrylic; 109 yards/50g): Ivory 24162, 1 ball

NEEDLES
US 7 (4.5mm) DPNs and 16 inch circular needles, or size to obtain gauge

NOTIONS
Yarn Needle
Stitch markers

GAUGE
20 sts and 26 rows – 4" stockinette stitch, blocked

Sea Urchin Washcloth

Notes:

This washcloth is worked in the round from the center outward.

M3B (Make 3 stitch bobble)

K1 to the front, K1 to back of same stitch, K1 to the front. Results in three stitches in one stitch. Turn work, P these three stitches. Turn work, K the three stitches. Turn work, P the three stitches. Turn work, starting with stitch three and working one stitch at a time, pass stitches three and two over stitch one.

M5B (Make 5 stitch bobble)

(K1 to the front, K1 to back of same stitch) two times, K1 to the front. Results in five stitches in one stitch. Turn work, P these five stitches. Turn work, K the five stitches. Turn work, P the five stitches. Turn work, starting with stitch five and working one stitch at a time, pass stitches five to two over stitch one.

Circular Cast On

Pinch the working yarn between the first and middle finger of your left hand so the end of the yarn comes out behind your fingers. Wrap the working yarn tail around the ring and pinky fingers of your left hand, holding the yarn tail firmly with your right hand. Point the tips of these fingers down toward your palm. *Using your right hand, insert the point of your needle (you can use double points or a circular) under the yarn across the back of your ring and pinky fingers (the 'first loop') from front to back. Pass the needle over the working yarn and draw a loop out from under the first loop; this creates one cast-on stitch. YO.* Repeat from * until you have cast on the required number of stitches. Note: If you need an even number of stitches, you will need to cast on the final stitch as a standard yarn over when you begin your first round of knitting. Arrange the stitches on your double point needles to begin knitting in the round. Tug on the yarn tail to draw the stitches into a tighter circle leaving a one inch diameter hole at center.

DIRECTIONS

Cast on 16 stitches using DPNs and Circular Cast On. Knit one round.

Row 1: *K1, M1, K1, M1, PM*, rep from * to * 8 times. (32 sts)

Row 2 and all even rows: K all stitches.

Row 3: K all sts.

Row 5: *K1, M1, K1, M3B, K1, M1, SM*, rep from * to * 8 times. (48 sts)

Row 7: K all sts.

Row 9: *K1, M1, K5, M1, SM*, rep from * to * 8 times. (64 sts)

Row 11: K all sts.

Row 13: *K1, M1, K3, M3B, K3, M1, SM*, rep from * to * 8 times. (80sts)

Row 15: K all sts.

Row 17: *K1, M1, M3B, K7, M3B, M1, SM*, rep from * to * 8 times. (96 sts)

Row 19: K all sts.

Row 21: *K1, M1, K5, M5B, K5, M1, SM*, rep from * to * 8 times. (112 sts)

Row 23: K all sts.

Row 25: *K1, M1, K2, M3B, K7, M3B, K2, M1, SM*, rep from * to * 8 times. (128 sts)

Row 27: K all sts.

Row 29: *K1, M1, K7, M5B, K7, M1, SM*, rep from * to * 8 times. (144 sts)

Row 31: K all sts.

Finishing

Bind off loosely. Weave in ends and block to finished measurements.

SAND AND SEA
SEA STAR HAND TOWEL

FINISHED MEASUREMENTS
11.75" wide X 20.5" long

YARN
Knit Picks Comfy Worsted (75% Pima Cotton, 25% Acrylic; 109 yards/50g): Color A Marina 25768, Color B Sea Foam 24153, Color C Ivory 24162, 1 ball each

NEEDLES
US 7 (4.5mm) DPNs and 16 inch or longer circular needles, or size to obtain gauge
Size I (5.5 mm) crochet hook

NOTIONS
Yarn Needle
Stitch markers
Waste yarn

GAUGE
20 sts and 26 rows = 4" stockinette stitch, blocked.

Sea Star Hand Towel

Notes:

This is worked in two halves. Stitches are cast on using a Provisional Cast On. The body and first ruffle are then worked as instructed. Then the waste yarn of the cast on is removed, the stitches placed on the needles, and the second ruffle worked the same as the first ruffle.

Provisional Cast On (Crochet Chain method)

Using a crochet hook several sizes too big for the yarn, make a slipknot and chain for 1". Hold knitting needle in left hand. With yarn in back of the needle, work next chain st by pulling the yarn over the needle and through the chain st. Move yarn under and behind needle, and repeat for the number of sts required. Chain a few more sts off the needle, then break yarn and pull end through last chain. CO sts will be incorrectly mounted; knit into the back of these sts. To unravel (when sts need to be picked up), pull chain end out, and the chain should unravel, leaving live sts. For video and photo tutorials for the Knitted Cast On, visit the Knit Picks website at http://www.knitpicks.com/tutorials.

Circular Cast On

Pinch the working yarn between the first and middle finger of your left hand so the end of the yarn comes out behind your fingers. Wrap the working yarn tail around the ring and pinky fingers of your left hand, holding the yarn tail firmly with your right hand. Point the tips of these fingers down toward your palm. *Using your right hand, insert the point of your needle (you can use double points or a circular) under the yarn across the back of your ring and pinky fingers (the 'first loop') from front to back. Pass the needle over the working yarn and draw a loop out from under the first loop; this creates one cast-on stitch. YO.* Repeat from * until you have cast on the required number of stitches. Note: If you need an even number of stitches, you will need to cast on the final stitch as a standard yarn over when you begin your first round of knitting. Arrange the stitches on your double point needles to begin knitting in the round. Tug on the yarn tail to draw the stitches into a tighter circle leaving a one inch diameter hole at center.

DIRECTIONS

Set up rows:
Cast on 59 stitches in Color B using a Provisional Cast On.
Turn and K1, P1, K1, P1, K1, P to last 5 sts, K1, P1, K1, P1, K1.

Body Instructions

Stripes
Continue in Color B.
Row 1: K1, P1, K1, P1, K1, K to last 4 sts, P1, K1, P1, K1.
Row 2: K1, P1, K1, P1, K1, P to last 5 sts, K1, P1, K1, P1, K1.

Change to Color C.
Row 3: K1, P1, K1, P1, K1, K to last 4 sts, P1, K1, P1, K1.
Row 4: K1, P1, K1, P1, K1, P to last 5 sts, K1, P1, K1, P1, K1.

Change to Color B.
Row 5: K1, P1, K1, P1, K1, K to last 4 sts, P1, K1, P1, K1.
Row 6: K1, P1, K1, P1, K1, P to last 5 sts, K1, P1, K1, P1, K1.

Change to Color C.
Row 7: K1, P1, K1, P1, K1, K to last 4 sts, P1, K1, P1, K1.
Row 8: K1, P1, K1, P1, K1, P to last 5 sts, K1, P1, K1, P1, K1.
Row 9: K1, P1, K1, P1, K1, K to last 4 sts, P1, K1, P1, K1.
Row 10: K1, P1, K1, P1, K1, P to last 5 sts, K1, P1, K1, P1, K1.
Row 11: K1, P1, K1, P1, K1, K to last 4 sts, P1, K1, P1, K1.
Row 12: K1, P1, K1, P1, K1, P to last 5 sts, K1, P1, K1, P1, K1.

Change to Color B.
Row 13: K1, P1, K1, P1, K1, K to last 4 sts, P1, K1, P1, K1.
Row 14: K1, P1, K1, P1, K1, P to last 5 sts, K1, P1, K1, P1, K1.

Change to Color C.
Row 15: K1, P1, K1, P1, K1, K to last 4 sts, P1, K1, P1, K1.
Row 16: K1, P1, K1, P1, K1, P to last 5 sts, K1, P1, K1, P1, K1.

Solid Body
Switch to Color B.
Repeat Rows 1 and 2 until piece measures 15.5 inches from cast on edge.

Second stripes Set
Change to Color C.
Row 1: K1, P1, K1, P1, K1, K to last 4 sts, P1, K1, P1, K1.
Row 2: K1, P1, K1, P1, K1, P to last 5 sts, K1, P1, K1, P1, K1.

Change to Color B.
Row 3: K1, P1, K1, P1, K1, K to last 4 sts, P1, K1, P1, K1.
Row 4: K1, P1, K1, P1, K1, P to last 5 sts, K1, P1, K1, P1, K1.

Change to Color C.
Row 5: K1, P1, K1, P1, K1, K to last 4 sts, P1, K1, P1, K1.
Row 6: K1, P1, K1, P1, K1, P to last 5 sts, K1, P1, K1, P1, K1.
Row 7: K1, P1, K1, P1, K1, K to last 4 sts, P1, K1, P1, K1.
Row 8: K1, P1, K1, P1, K1, P to last 5 sts, K1, P1, K1, P1, K1.
Row 9: K1, P1, K1, P1, K1, K to last 4 sts, P1, K1, P1, K1.
Row 10: K1, P1, K1, P1, K1, P to last 5 sts, K1, P1, K1, P1, K1.

Change to Color B.
Row 11: K1, P1, K1, P1, K1, K to last 4 sts, P1, K1, P1, K1.
Row 12: K1, P1, K1, P1, K1, P to last 5 sts, K1, P1, K1, P1, K1.

Change to Color C.
Row 13: K1, P1, K1, P1, K1, K to last 4 sts, P1, K1, P1, K1.
Row 14: K1, P1, K1, P1, K1, P to last 5 sts, K1, P1, K1, P1, K1.

Change to Color B.
Row 15: K1, P1, K1, P1, K1, K to last 4 sts, P1, K1, P1, K1.
Row 16: K1, P1, K1, P1, K1, P to last 5 sts, K1, P1, K1, P1, K1.
Row 17: K1, P1, K1, P1, K1, K to last 4 sts, P1, K1, P1, K1.
Row 18: K1, P1, K1, P1, K1, P to last 5 sts, K1, P1, K1, P1, K1.

Ruffled Edge

Change to Color C.
Row 1: K2, *KFB, K1*, rep from * to * 28 times, K1. (87sts).
Row 2: K2, P to last two stitches, K2.
Row 3: K all sts.
Row 4: K2, P to last two stitches, K2.
Repeat Rows 3 and 4 two more times.

Change to Color B.
K two rows. Loosely bind off all stitches.

Second Half of Body:

Remove Provisional Cast On, placing resulting live stitches onto needle. Using Color C, attach yarn in first stitch to the right with RS of the wrap facing you. Work Ruffled Edge as described above then make the sea stars.

Sea Stars

(make 6 - 3 for each side)

Body:

Cast on 8 stitches onto DPNs in Color A using Circular Cast On. K all sts.

Row 1: *K1, M1*, rep from * to * eight times. (16 sts).

Row 2: K all sts.

Row 3: *K1, M1, K1*, rep from * to * eight times. (24 sts).

Row 4: K1, M1, K23. (25 sts)

Legs (5 for each Sea Star)

Each leg is worked separately.

Separate body into five sections of five stitches. Keeping first five stitches on the needles, place the remaining 20 sts on waste yarn.

Row 1: K all sts.

Row 2: Turn and P all sts.

Row 3: K1, SL 2, K1, P2SSO, K1.

Row 4: P all sts.

Row 5: SL 2, K1, P2SSO.

Cut thread and pull through remaining stitch.

Place the next 5 sts on the needles. Repeat the instructions on how to work leg until you have five legs.

Finishing

Weave in ends and block, laying the body and sea stars flat to dry and ruffling the ends of the towel. Sew sea stars onto striped sections.

SAND AND SEA
SEA SNAIL BATH MAT

FINISHED MEASUREMENTS
22" diameter

YARN
Knit Picks Comfy Worsted (75% Pima Cotton, 25% Acrylic; 109 yards/50g): Color A Marina 25768, 2 balls; Color B Sea Foam 24153, 4 balls; Color C Ivory 24162, 2 balls

NEEDLES
US 7 (4.5mm) DPNs and circular needles, or size to obtain gauge

NOTIONS
Yarn Needle
Removable Stitch markers

GAUGE
20 sts and 26 rows = 4" stockinette stitch

Sea Snail Bath Mat

Notes:

This bath mat is knit in a spiral from the inside out. Each spiral is worked over ten stitches and is joined to the inner spiral as you knit. The spiral is achieved by short row shaping.

Using DPNs is easiest to start the mat, due to the amount of stitches,

Weave in ends as you work.

Wrap & Turn:

Work until the st to be wrapped. If knitting: Bring yarn to the front of the work, sl next st as if to P, return the yarn to the back; turn work and slip wrapped st onto RH needle. Continue across row. If purling: Bring yarn to the back of the work, sl next st as if to P, return the yarn to the front; turn work and slip wrapped st onto RH needle. Continue across row.

Picking up wraps: Work to the wrapped st. If knitting, insert the RH needle under the wrap(s), then through the wrapped st K-wise. K the wrap(s) together with the wrapped st. If purling, slip the wrapped st P-wise onto the RH needle, and use the LH needle to lift the wrap(s) and place them on the RH needle. Slip wrap(s) and unworked st back to LH needle; purl all together through the back loop.

DIRECTIONS
Inner Spiral

Cast on 10 sts using Color A and a long-tail cast on. K all sts.

Row 1: SL 1, K8, W&T.

Row 2 and all even rows: K all sts.

Row 3: SL 1, K7, W&T.

Row 5: SL 1, K6, W&T.

Row 7: SL 1, K5, W&T.

Row 9: SL 1, K4, W&T.

Row 11: SL 1, K3, W&T.

Row 13: SL 1, K2, W&T.

Row 15: SL 1, K1, W&T.

Switch to Color B.

Row 17: K all sts.

Rows 19 – 34: repeat Rows 1 – 16.

Switch to Color C.

Row 35: K all sts.

Rows 37 – 52: repeat Rows 1 – 16.

Switch to Color B.

Row 53: SL 1, K8, W&T.

Row 55: SL 1, K7, W&T.

Row 57: SL 1, K6, W&T.

Row 59: SL 1, K5, W&T.

Row 61: SL 1, K4, W&T.

Row 63: SL 1, K8, SL 1, pick up and knit first st along edge of cast on row, PSSO.

Switch to Color A.

Row 65: SL 1, K8, SL 1, pick up and knit third st along edge of cast on row, PSSO.

Rows 67 –76: repeat Rows 53 – 62.

Row 77: SL 1, K8, SL 1, pick up and knit fourth st along edge of cast on row, PSSO.

Switch to Color B.

Row 79: SL 1, K8, SL 1, pick up and knit sixth st along edge of cast on row, PSSO.

Rows 81 – 90: repeat rows 53 – 62.

Row 91: SL 1, K8, SL 1, pick up and knit seventh st along edge of cast on row, PSSO.

Switch to Color C.

Row 93: SL 1, K8, SL 1, pick up and knit ninth st along edge of cast on row, PSSO.

Rows 95 – 104: repeat Rows 53 – 62.

Row 105: SL 1, K8, SL 1, pick up and knit tenth st along edge of cast on row, PSSO.

Row 106: K all sts.

Outer spirals

You have now completed the beginning of the spiral of the shell. From this point you will be working the spiral in rounds around the entire spiral. Place removable stitch marker around first stitch on the needles to mark the beginning of the round.

Color changes: When starting Round 1, switch to Color B. For the rest of Round 1 and all remaining Rounds, switch color every 12 rows in the color pattern of: *Color C, Color B, Color A, Color B*, repeat from * to * as needed over length of mat. This should result in six garter ridges of each color before changing to the next color.

Round 1

Row 1: SL 1, K8, W&T.

Row 2 and all even rows: K all sts.

Row 3: SL 1, K8, SL 1, pick up and knit the next stitch from spiral edge, PSSO.

Repeat Rows 1 – 4 until you reach the marker. Reposition the removable stitch marker around first stitch on the needles to mark the beginning of the round. Begin Round 2.

Round 2

Row 1: SL 1, K8, W&T.

Row 2 and all even rows: K all sts.

Row 3: SL 1, K8, SL 1, pick up and knit the next stitch from spiral edge, PSSO.

Row 5: SL 1, K8, SL 1, pick up and knit the next stitch from spiral edge, PSSO.

Repeat Rows 1 – 6 until you reach the marker. Reposition the removable stitch marker around first stitch on the needles to mark the beginning of the round. Begin Round 3.

Round 3

Row 1: SL 1, K8, W&T.

Row 2 and all even rows: K all sts.

Row 3: SL 1, K8, SL 1, pick up and knit the next stitch from spiral edge, PSSO.

Row 5: SL 1, K8, SL 1, pick up and knit the next stitch from spiral edge, PSSO.

Row 7: SL 1, K8, SL 1, pick up and knit the next stitch from spiral edge, PSSO.

Repeat Rows 1 – 8 until you reach the marker. Reposition the removable stitch marker around first stitch on the needles to mark the beginning of the round. Begin Round 4.

Round 4
Row 1: SL 1, K8, W&T.
Row 2 and all even rows: K all sts.
Row 3: SL 1, K8, SL 1, pick up and knit the next stitch from spiral edge, PSSO.
Row 5: SL 1, K8, SL 1, pick up and knit the next stitch from spiral edge, PSSO.
Row 7: SL 1, K8, SL 1, pick up and knit the next stitch from spiral edge, PSSO.
Row 9: SL 1, K8, SL 1, pick up and knit the next stitch from spiral edge, PSSO.

Repeat Rows 1 – 10 until you reach the marker. Reposition the removable stitch marker around first stitch on the needles to mark the beginning of the round. Begin Round 5.

Round 5
Place a second removable stitch marker on the edge stitch halfway around the round, directly across from first stitch marker.
Row 1: S1, K8, W&T.
Row 2 and all even rows: K all sts.
Row 3: SL 1, K8, SL 1, pick up and knit the next stitch from spiral edge, PSSO.
Row 5: SL 1, K8, SL 1, pick up and knit the next stitch from spiral

edge, PSSO.
Row 7: SL 1, K8, SL 1, pick up and knit the next stitch from spiral edge, PSSO.
Row 9: SL 1, K8, SL 1, pick up and knit the next stitch from spiral edge, PSSO.
Row 11: SL 1, K8, SL 1, pick up and knit the next stitch from spiral edge, PSSO.

Repeat Rows 1 – 12 until you reach the second stitch marker. Begin the shell opening.

Shell Opening
Color Changes: Continue alternating colors as described for the outer spiral above.

Row 1: SL 1, K to last st, W&T.
Row 2 and all even rows: K all sts.
Row 3: SL 1, M1, K to last st, SL 1, pick up and knit the next stitch from spiral edge, PSSO. 1 st inc.
Row 5: SL 1, K to last st, SL 1, pick up and knit the next stitch from spiral edge, PSSO.
Row 7: SL 1, M1, K to last st, SL 1, pick up and knit the next stitch from spiral edge, PSSO. 1 st inc.
Row 9: SL 1, K to last st, SL 1, pick up and knit the next stitch from spiral edge, PSSO.
Row 11: SL 1, M1, K to last st, SL 1, pick up and knit the next stitch from spiral edge, PSSO. 1 st inc.
Repeat Rows 1 – 12 until you have 31 stitches on the needles.

Finishing
Bind off all stitches. Weave in remaining ends. Block, lay flat to dry.

Rejuvenating Waves Spa Set

Relax into the waves with this three piece spa set featuring a face towel, spa cloth and a soap pouch. All designed to pamper you with the gentle touch of soft cotton. Using simple shells of alternating heights give these pieces a beautiful personal addition to your space.

Happy Crocheting!

Beth Major

REJUVENATING WAVES
SPA CLOTH

FINISHED MEASUREMENTS
9.5" Square

YARN
Knit Picks Dishie (100% Cotton; 190 yards/100g): Linen 25400 (Color A), 1 balls, Kenai 25788 (Color B), 1 ball

HOOKS
US G-6 (4 mm) crochet hook or size to obtain gauge

NOTIONS
Yarn Needle

GAUGE
15 sts and 8 rows = 4" in DC, lightly blocked

Spa Cloth

Notes:

Stitches of varying heights alternating with simple shells create the beautiful wavy patterns in this spa cloth.

Special Terms

Foundation Single Crochet (FSC)

CH 2, insert hook into first CH, YO and pull up loop, YO and pull through one loop (CH 1 made), YO and pull through both loops (SC made). *Insert hook into CH just made, YO and pull up a loop, YO and pull through one loop (CH 1 made), YO and pull through both loops (SC made)* Repeat from * to* as many times as required.

Shell

5 DC in indicated ST.

Crab Stitch (Reverse Single Crochet):

Right Handed – without turning work you will be working the SC in the opposite direction of your normal direction, (insert hook into ST to the right of your current ST, YO and pull up a loop, YO and pull through both loops) repeat as instructed.

Left Handed – without turning work you will be working the SC in the opposite direction of your normal direction, (insert hook into ST to the left of your current ST, YO and pull up a loop, YO and pull through both loops) repeat as instructed.

DIRECTIONS

Row 1: With Color A, FSC 31.

Row 2: Continuing with Color A, CH 1, turn, SC in first ST, (HDC in next ST, DC in next ST, TR in next ST, DC in next ST, HDC in next ST, SC in next ST), repeat across to end of row.

Row 3: CH 3, 2 DC in first SC, SC in next TR, (Shell in next SC, SC in next TR), repeat across to last 3 STS, 3 DC in last sc.

Row 4: CH 1, turn, SC in BLP of first ST, working in BLO (HDC in next ST, DC in next ST, TR in next ST, DC in next ST, HDC in next ST, SC in next ST), repeat across to end of row.

Row 5: Switch to Color B, repeat Row 3.

Row 6: Switch to Color A, repeat Row 4.

Row 7: Repeat Row 5.

Row 8: Repeat Row 6.

Continuing in Color A, repeat Rows 3 and 4 until cloth measures approximately 9-9.5" finishing at the end of a Row 4.

Finishing

Edging

Rnd 1: Switch to Color B, CH 1, do not turn, 3 SC in corner, work 31 SC evenly along side of square, 3 SC in next corner, work SC in each CH across bottom of foundation row, 3 SC in corner, work 31 SC evenly up next side of square, 3 SC in corner, work SC in each ST across, Join last ST to first ST with a SL ST, CH 1.

Rnd 2: Continuing with Color B, do not turn, work reverse SC (Crab Stitch) in each SC around. Join last ST to first ST with a SL ST. Fasten off.

Weave in ends and block to size.

REJUVENATING WAVES
FACE TOWEL

FINISHED MEASUREMENTS
16" by 26"

YARN
Knit Picks Dishie (100% Cotton; 190 yards/100g): Linen 25400 (Color A), 1 ball, Kenai 25788 (Color B), 1 ball

HOOKS
US G-6 (4 mm) crochet hook or size to obtain gauge

NOTIONS
Yarn Needle

GAUGE
15 sts and 8 rows = 4" in DC, lightly blocked

Face Towel

Notes:

Stitches of varying heights alternating with simple shells create the beautiful wavy patterns in this large face towel.

Special Terms

Foundation Single Crochet (FSC)

CH 2, insert hook into first CH, YO and pull up loop, YO and pull through one loop (CH 1 made), YO and pull through both loops (SC made). *Insert hook into CH just made, YO and pull up a loop, YO and pull through one loop (CH 1 made), YO and pull through both loops (SC made)* Repeat from * to* as many times as required.

Shell

5 DC in indicated ST.

Crab Stitch (Reverse Single Crochet):

Right Handed – without turning work you will be working the SC in the opposite direction of your normal direction, (insert hook into ST to the right of your current ST, YO and pull up a loop, YO and pull through both loops) repeat as instructed.

Left Handed – without turning work you will be working the SC in the opposite direction of your normal direction, (insert hook into ST to the left of your current ST, YO and pull up a loop, YO and pull through both loops) repeat as instructed.

DIRECTIONS

Row 1: With Color A, FSC 103.

Row 2: Continuing with Color A, CH 1, turn, SC in first ST, (HDC in next ST, DC in next ST, TR in next ST, DC in next ST, HDC in next ST, SC in next ST), repeat across to end of row.

Row 3: CH 3, 2 DC in first SC, SC in next TR, (Shell in next SC, SC in next TR), repeat across to last 3 STS, 3 DC in last sc.

Row 4: CH 1, turn, SC in BLP of first ST, working in BLO (HDC in next ST, DC in next ST, TR in next ST, DC in next ST, HDC in next ST, SC in next ST), repeat across to end of row.

Row 5: Switch to Color B, repeat Row 3.

Row 6: Switch to Color A, repeat Row 4.

Row 7 to 12: Repeat Row 5 and 6

Continuing in Color A, repeat Rows 3 and 4 until cloth measures approximately 15.5-16" finishing at the end of a Row 4.

Finishing

Edging

Rnd 1: Switch to Color B, CH 1, do not turn, 3 SC in corner, work 62 SC evenly along side of square, 3 SC in next corner, work SC in each CH across bottom of foundation row, 3 SC in corner, work 62 SC evenly up next side of square, 3 SC in corner, work SC in each ST across, Join last ST to first ST with a SL ST, CH 1.

Rnd 2: Continuing with Color B, do not turn, work reverse SC (Crab Stitch) in each SC around. Join last ST to first ST with a SL ST. Fasten off.

Weave in ends and block to size.

REJUVENATING WAVES
SOAP POUCH

FINISHED MEASUREMENTS
3.5" by 4.5"

YARN
Knit Picks Dishie (100% Cotton; 190 yards/100g): Linen 25400 (Color A), 1 ball. Kenai 25788 (Color B), 1 ball

HOOKS
US G-6 (4 mm) crochet hook or size to obtain gauge

NOTIONS
Yarn Needle

GAUGE
15 sts and 8 rows = 4" in DC, lightly blocked

Soap Pouch.

Notes:

Stitches of varying heights alternating with simple shells create the beautiful wavy patterns in this cute soap pouch.

Special Terms

Foundation Single Crochet (FSC)

CH 2, insert hook into first CH, YO and pull up loop, YO and pull through one loop (CH 1 made), YO and pull through both loops (SC made). *Insert hook into CH just made, YO and pull up a loop, YO and pull through one loop (CH 1 made), YO and pull through both loops (SC made)* Repeat from * to* as many times as required.

Shell

5 DC in indicated ST.

Crab Stitch (Reverse Single Crochet):

Right Handed – without turning work you will be working the SC in the opposite direction of your normal direction, (insert hook into ST to the right of your current ST, YO and pull up a loop, YO and pull through both loops) repeat as instructed.

Left Handed – without turning work you will be working the SC in the opposite direction of your normal direction, (insert hook into ST to the left of your current ST, YO and pull up a loop, YO and pull through both loops) repeat as instructed.

DIRECTIONS

Row 1: With Color A, FSC 13.

Row 2: Mark as Right side, CH 4, turn, TR in first ST, (DC in next ST, HDC in next ST, SC in next ST, HDC in next ST, DC in next ST, TR in next ST) repeat once.

Row 3: Switch to Color B, CH 1, turn, SC in first TR, (Shell in next SC, SC in next TR) repeat once.

Row 4: Switch to Color A, CH 4, turn, working in BLO across row, TR in first SC, (DC in next ST, HDC in next ST, SC in next ST, HDC in next ST, DC in next ST, TR in next SC) repeat once.

Rows 5 & 6: Repeat Rows 3 and 4.

Rows 7 to 10: Continue with Color A only and repeat Rows 3 and 4.

Row 11: Switch to Color B, CH 3, DC in first st, CH 1, (sk next st, DC in next st, CH 1) repeat across.

Fasten off. Go to Finishing.

Finishing

Rnd 1: With Wrong sides together and the stripes lined up, insert hook through both pieces at top left corner (top right if you are left handed) just below the final row of DC's and join Color B with a SL ST, CH 1, SC in same st, work 17 sc evenly down side of bag, 3 SC in corner, SC in each CH across foundation row, 3SC in corner, work 18 SC evenly up next side of bag finishing with last st just under the final row of DC.

Rnd 2: Continuing with Color B, ch 1, do not turn, work reverse SC (Crab Stitch) in each SC around. Fasten off.

Weave in ends and block to size.

Soap Pouch Loop

Step 1: With Color B, FSC 16.

Step 2: Place either end of the work on the front and back of 1 corner of the Soap Bag. Insert hook through the Soap Bag and through the first ST of the FSC, YO and pull through a loop, CH 1, SC into same space, CH 1 and fasten off. Weave in ends.

A Little Bit of Lace Bath Set

A Little Bit of Lace Bath Set is a fun and easy knit, and only uses two skeins of Dishie for the entire set. It contains a facecloth, hanging towel, and soap sachet. Each piece features the same lace pattern used as a border, a repeating pattern, or as an all-over design. Perfect to pamper yourself with, or give as a thoughtful gift.

Happy Knitting!

Faith Schmidt

A LITTLE BIT OF LACE
FACE CLOTH

FINISHED MEASUREMENTS
10 x 11", blocked

YARN
Knit Picks Dishie (100% Cotton; 190 yards/100g): Swan 25409, 1 ball.

NEEDLES
US 5 (3.75mm) straight or circular needles, or size to obtain gauge.

NOTIONS
Yarn Needle

GAUGE
16.5 sts = 4" in St st, unblocked.

Face Cloth

Notes:

Yardage: While the whole set can be made with two coordinating colors of Dishie, here are the yardages for each piece individually. Cloth: 85 yards of C1, Hanging Towel: 30 yards of C1 and 115 yards of C2, Soap Sachet: 30 yards each of C1 and C2. The total yardage for C1 and C2 is approximately 145 yards each.

Gauge: Make sure to knit a gauge swatch to determine what size you needle you need to use to get the specified gauge. I tend to knit loosely, so you may have to go up a needle size or two to obtain gauge.

Resizing: To resize the Cloth, use a multiple of 6+4 sts.

Double Vertical Decrease (DVD)
Sl 2 sts K-wise, K1, pass both sl sts over the knit st and off the needle. 2 sts dec.

Full Lace Stitch (worked flat over multiples of 6 sts plus 4)
Row 1 (RS): K2, *K3, YO, DVD, YO, rep from * to last 2 sts, K2.
Row 2 (WS): K2, P to last 2 sts, K2.
Row 3: K2, *YO, DVD, YO, K3, rep from * to last 2 sts, K2.
Row 4: Rep Row 2.
Rep Rows 1-4 for pattern.

Edge Lace Stitch (worked flat)
Row 1 (RS): K to last 5 sts, YO, DVD, YO, K2.
Row 2 (WS): K2, P to last 2 sts, K2.
Row 3: K2, YO, DVD, YO, K to end.
Row 4: Rep Row 2.
Rep Rows 1-4 for pattern.

DIRECTIONS

CO 40 sts, using the Long Tail CO.

Knit 2 rows.

Work Rows 1-4 of Full Lace Stitch two times.

Work Rows 1-4 of Edge Lace Stitch until piece measures 10", or desired length from CO, ending with a WS row.

Rep Rows 1-4 of Full Lace Stitch two times, ending with a Row 3 on the second repeat.

Knit 2 rows.

BO on the WS, K-wise.

Finishing
Weave in ends and block as desired.

A LITTLE BIT OF LACE
HANGING TOWEL

FINISHED MEASUREMENTS
12.5 x 17" with strap buttoned, blocked

YARN
Knit Picks Dishie (100% Cotton; 190 yards/100g): C1 Swan 25409, C2: Azure 25412, 1 ball each

NEEDLES
US 4 (3.5mm) straight or circular needles, or size to obtain gauge

NOTIONS
Yarn Needle
5/8" Button

GAUGE
18 sts = 4" in St st, unblocked.

Hanging Towel

Notes:

Gauge: Make sure to knit a gauge swatch to determine what size you needle you need to use to get the specified gauge. I tend to knit loosely, so you may have to go up a needle size or two to obtain gauge.

Double Vertical Decrease (DVD)
Sl 2 sts K-wise, K1, pass both sl sts over the knit st and off the needle. 2 sts dec.

Full Lace Stitch (worked flat over multiples of 6 sts plus 4)
Row 1 (RS): K2, *K3, YO, DVD, YO, rep from * to last 2 sts, K2.
Row 2 (WS): K2, P to last 2 sts, K2.
Row 3: K2, *YO, DVD, YO, K3, rep from * to last 2 sts, K2.
Row 4: Rep Row 2.
Rep Rows 1-4 for pattern.

Edge Lace Stitch (worked flat)
Row 1 (RS): K to last 5 sts, YO, DVD, YO, K2.
Row 2 (WS): K2, P to last 2 sts, K2.
Row 3: K2, YO, DVD, YO, K to end.
Row 4: Rep Row 2.
Rep Rows 1-4 for pattern.

DIRECTIONS

With C2, CO 52 sts, using the Long Tail CO.

Knit 2 rows.

Work Rows 1-4 of Full Lace Stitch two times.

Work Rows 1-4 of Edge Lace Stitch four times.

Repeat these two sections three more times, for a total of four repeats. On the last repeat of the Edge Lace Stitch work only one repeal.

Change to C1 and knit 2 rows.

Decrease on next row as follows (RS): K6, *K2tog, repeat from * to last 6 sts, K6. (32 sts).

Knit 3 rows.

Decrease Section
Row 1 (RS): K1, SSK, K to last 3 sts, K2tog, K1. 2 sts dec.
Row 2 (WS): Knit.

Repeat Decrease Section a total of 11 times, until 10 sts remain.

Next Row (RS): K4, K2tog, K4. (9 sts).

Knit 25 Rows.

Work Buttonhole Row as follows (RS): K4, YO, K2tog, K3.

Knit 7 Rows.

BO all sts.

Finishing
Sew button to inside of strap, 4" from end of strap. weave in ends and block to size.

A LITTLE BIT OF LACE
SOAP SACHET

FINISHED MEASUREMENTS
3" x 7", unblocked

YARN
Knit Picks Dishie (100% Cotton; 190 yards/100g): C1 Swan 25409, C2: Azure 25412, 1 ball each

NEEDLES
US 4 (3.5mm) DPNs or two 24" circular needles for two circulars technique, or one 32" or longer circular needle for Magic Loop technique, or size to obtain gauge

NOTIONS
Yarn Needle

GAUGE
20 sts = 4" in St st, in the round unblocked

Soap Sachet

Notes:

Gauge: Make sure to knit a gauge swatch to determine what size you needle you need to use to get the specified gauge. I tend to knit loosely, so you may have to go up a needle size or two to obtain gauge.

Resizing: To resize the Soap Sachet, use a multiple of 6 sts.

Double Vertical Decrease (DVD)
Sl 2 sts K-wise, K1, pass both sl sts over the knit st and off the needle. 2 sts dec.

I-Cord
CO 3 sts. *Knit a row. Slide row to other end of needle without turning work. Pull yarn firmly and repeat from *, creating a tube.

Lace Stitch (in the round over multiples of 6 sts)
Rnd 1: K3, YO, DVD, YO.
Rnd 2: Knit.
Rnd 3: YO, DVD, YO, K3.
Rnd 4: Knit.
Rep Rounds 1-4 for pattern.

DIRECTIONS

With C2, CO 24 sts, using the Long Tail CO. Using your preferred method of knitting in the round, and being careful not to twist the sts, PM and join to knit in the round.

Knit 8 rounds.

Change to C1, and work reps of Lace Stitch in the Round until piece measures 5.75" from CO.

Change to C2 and knit 8 rounds.

BO.

I-Cord Ties (Make 2)
With smaller needles, and C2, knit a 3 st I-Cord until it measures 9".

BO all sts.

Finishing
Weave I-Cord through the first row of the lace section on each end of the Soap Sachet, and tie. The Soap Sachet doesn't need to be blocked.

Mirror Lattice Spa Set

If cables are the epitome of cozy, reversible cables are pure bliss! The Mirror Lattice Spa Set is a wonderful way to pamper a loved one, or a plush indulgence for yourself. All three pieces knit up quickly in an easy-to-memorize stitch pattern that is well within reach of adventurous beginners. The ruffled washcloth is the perfect hostess or shower gift when paired with a bar of handmade soap, or create a care package for a loved one with the headband, hand towel, and washcloth. The 100% cotton yarn can be washed and dried and just gets softer with use.

Happy Knitting!

Kendra Nitta

MIRROR LATTICE

HAND TOWEL

FINISHED MEASUREMENTS
Approx 7.5" x 21", blocked

YARN
Knit Picks Dishie (100% Cotton; 190 yards/100g): Eggplant 27039, 3 balls

NEEDLES
US 7 (4.5mm) straight or circular needles, or size to obtain gauge

NOTIONS
Cable Needle

GAUGE
36 sts and 29 rows = 4" in Mirror Lattice pattern, unblocked. (Gauge for this project is approximate)

Hand Towel

Notes:

Reversible cables make this pretty hand towel extra absorbent. Working the cables at the beginning and end of Row 1 can be a bit tricky at first, but worth the effort to master for the lovely edging it creates.

Seed Stitch (worked flat over an even number of stitches)
Row 1 (RS): (K1, P1) to end.
Row 2 (WS): (P1, K1) to end.
Repeat Rows 1 and 2 for pattern.

4/4RRC
Sl4 to CN, hold to back, (K1, P1) twice; (K1, P1) twice from CN
4/4LRC
Sl4 to CN, hold to front, (K1, P1) twice; (K1, P1) twice from CN

Mirror Lattice (worked flat over 24 sts)
Adapted from the Telescope Lattice stitch pattern in A Second Treasury of Knitting Patterns *by Barbara G. Walker*
Row 1 (RS): 4/4RRC, (K1, P1) 4 times, 4/4LRC.
Rows 2 (WS), 3, and 4: (K1, P1) to end.
Row 5: (K1, P1) twice, 4/4LRC, 4/4RRC, (K1, P1) twice.
Rows 6, 7, and 8: (K1, P1) to end.

Moss Stitch (worked flat over an even number of stitches)
Row 1 (RS): (P1, K1) to end.
Rows 2 (WS) and 3: (K1, P1) to end.
Row 4: (P1, K1) to end.

DIRECTIONS

CO 144 sts.

Work in Seed St for 4 rows.

Work Rows 1-8 of Mirror Lattice 3 times, then work Row 1 once more.

Decr row (WS): (SSK, P2tog) to end. 72 sts rem. Work in Moss St for 2 inches, ending with a RS row.

Incr row (WS): KFB to end. 144 sts. Work Rows 1 8 of Mirror Lattice 10 times, then work Row 1 once more.

Decr row (WS): (SSK, P2tog) to end. 72 sts rem.

Work in Moss St for 2 inches, ending with a RS row.

Incr row (WS): KFB to end. 144 sts.

Work Rows 1-8 of Mirror Lattice 3 times, then work Row 1 once more.

Work in Seed St for 4 rows.

BO loosely in patt.

Finishing

Weave in ends, wash and block to finished dimensions, using your fingers to define and distribute ruffles evenly at top and bottom.

MIRROR LATTICE

WASHCLOTH

FINISHED MEASUREMENTS
Approx 7.5″ square, blocked

YARN
Knit Picks Dishie (100% Cotton; 190 yards/100g): Lilac Mist 27038, 1 ball

NEEDLES
US 7 (4.5mm) straight or circular needles, or size to obtain gauge

NOTIONS
Cable Needle

GAUGE
36 sts and 29 rows = 4″ in Mirror Lattice pattern, unblocked. (Gauge for this project is approximate)

Washclot

Notes:

Ruffles and cables make this reversible washclot as pretty as it is practical. Working the cables at the beginning and end of Row 1 can be a bit tricky at first, but worth the effort to master for the lovely edging it creates.

Seed Stitch (worked flat over an even number of stitches)
Row 1 (RS): (K1, P1) to end.
Row 2 (WS): (P1, K1) to end
Repeat Rows 1 and 2 for pattern

4/4RRC
Sl4 to CN, hold to back, (K1, P1) twice; (K1, P1) twice from CN
4/4LRC
Sl4 to CN, hold to front, (K1, P1) twice; (K1, P1) twice from CN

Mirror Lattice (worked flat over 24 sts)
Adapted from the Telescope Lattice stitch pattern in A Second Treasury of Knitting Patterns *by Barbara G. Walker*
Row 1 (RS): 4/4RRC, (K1, P1) 4 times, 4/4LRC.
Rows 2 (WS), 3, and 4: (K1, P1) to end.
Row 5: (K1, P1) twice, 4/4LRC, 4/4RRC, (K1, P1) twice.
Rows 6, 7, and 8: (K1, P1) to end.

DIRECTIONS

CO 72 sts.

Work in Seed St for 4 rows.

Work Rows 1-8 of Mirror Lattice 6 times, then work Row 1 once more.

Next row (WS): Work in Seed St for 4 rows.

BO loosely in patt.

Finishing

Weave in ends, wash and block to finished dimensions, using your fingers to define and distribute ruffles evenly at top and bottom.

MIRROR LATTICE
HEADBAND

FINISHED MEASUREMENTS
2.5" wide x 16" circumference

YARN
Knit Picks Dishie (100% Cotton; 190 yards/100g): Swan 25409, 1 ball

NEEDLES
US 7 (4.5mm) straight or circular needles, or size to obtain gauge

NOTIONS
Cable Needle, Waste Yarn

GAUGE
24 sts and 18 rows = 2.5" in Mirror Lattice pattern, unblocked. (Gauge for this project is approximate)

Headband

Notes:

This pretty headband uses only about 60 yards-- perfect for those worsted leftovers you've been saving! Reversible cables make this project a plush, spa-like indulgence. The cable needle doubles as your spare needle for the 3-needle bind-off.

4/4RRC
Sl4 to CN, hold to back, (K1, P1) twice; (K1, P1) twice from CN

4/4LRC
Sl4 to CN, hold to front, (K1, P1) twice; (K1, P1) twice from CN

Mirror Lattice (worked flat over 24 sts)
Adapted from the Telescope Lattice stitch pattern in A Second Treasury of Knitting Patterns *by Barbara G. Walker*

Row 1 (RS): 4/4RRC, (K1, P1) 4 times, 4/4LRC.
Rows 2 (WS), 3, and 4: (K1, P1) to end.
Row 5: (K1, P1) twice, 4/4LRC, 4/4RRC, (K1, P1) twice.
Rows 6, 7, and 8: (K1, P1) to end.

Garter Stitch (worked flat)
All Rows: Knit all stitches

Provisional Cast On
For help casting on provisionally, please refer to the following tutorial:
http://tutorials.knitpicks.com/wptutorials/traditional-provisional/

3-Needle Bind Off
For information on 3-Needle Bind Off, please refer to the following tutorial.
http://tutorials.knitpicks.com/wptutorials/3-needle-bind-off/

DIRECTIONS

CO 6 sts using a provisional CO. Work in Garter St for 6 rows.

Inc row (RS): K1, KFB, K until 2 sts rem, KFB, K1. 8 sts.
Next row: K.
Rep these 2 rows twice more. 12 sts
Work in Garter St for 8 rows.

Next row (RS): (KFB) to end. 24 sts. (K1, P1) to end.

Work Rows 1-8 of Mirror Lattice 8 times, then work Rows 1 and 2 once more.

Next row (RS): (SSK) to end. 12 sts.

Work in Garter St for 7 rows.

Dec row (RS): K1, SSK, knit until 3 sts rem, K2TOG, K1. 10 sts
Next row: Knit.
Rep these 2 rows twice more. 6 sts

Work in Garter St until piece measures 16" from CO, or 5" less than head circumference, ending with a WS row.

Transfer sts from provisional CO to CN. With RS tog, BO using 3-needle BO.

Finishing
Weave in ends, wash and block to finished dimensions.

Breakfast of Champions Kitchen Set

If you would like to have breakfast on the table for every meal of the day, the Breakfast of Champions table set is perfect for you. If you're not in the mood for an omelet, have your eggs Sunny Side Up. Put a pat of butter on your Toast, add some Orange Slices, and you'll have a complete, nutritious breakfast in no time. Each piece offers a chance to fortify your knitting skills. The placemat is knit in the round from the center out and includes evenly spaced increases to form the circular egg shape. The napkin includes a touch of intarsia along each side to form the crust of the toast, and the cup cozy is worked in stranded knitting. Knit in a cotton/Modal® blend, the pieces are durable and can be easily laundered. Bon Appétit!

Happy Knitting!

Joyce Fassbender

BREAKFAST OF CHAMPIONS
BUTTERED TOAST NAPKIN

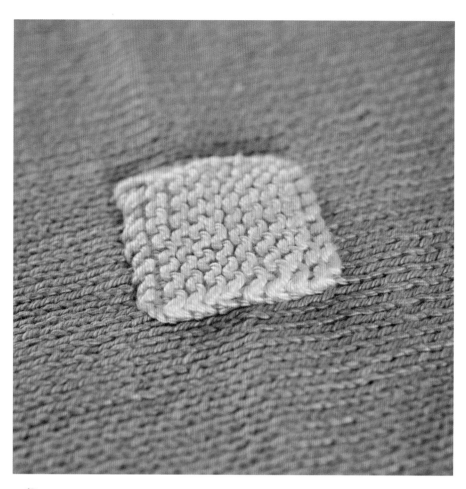

FINISHED MEASUREMENTS
10″x 12″

YARN
Knit Picks Shine Sport (60% Pima Cotton, 40% Modal®; 110 yards/50g): MC: Willow 23816; CC1: Coffee 27007; CC2: Dandelion 25340, 1 ball each

NEEDLES
US size 4 (3.5mm) needles, or size to obtain gauge

NOTIONS
Tapestry needle
Stitch markers

GAUGE
24 sts and 30 rows = 4″ stockinette stitch

Buttered Toast Napkin

Notes:

When changing colors, bring the new color up underneath the old color to prevent holes from forming at the sides of the napkin. To work the sides of the napkin, form a second ball of the CC1 (containing ~30 yards).

DIRECTIONS

Set Up Rows:

Cast on 60 sts in CC1 using long tail cast on.

Work four rows as: K all sts

Napkin Body:

Row 1: K3 in CC1, attach MC, K56 in MC, attach second ball of CC1, K3 in CC1

Row 2: K3 in CC1, (K2, P52, K2) in MC, K3 in CC1

Row 3: K3 in CC1, K56 in MC, K3 in CC1

Row 4: K3 in CC1, (K2, P52, K2) in MC, K3 in CC1

Repeat rows 3 and 4 until piece measures 11.5 inches.

Top Edge

Break MC and second ball of CC1. Using only one ball, in CC1, work five rows as: K all sts.

Bind off all sts. Make butter pat.

Butter pat (make one)

Cast on 9 sts in CC2.

Work 17 rows as: K all sts.

Bind off all sts.

Finishing

Weave in ends. Block and lay flat to dry. Sew butter pat to center of toast.

BREAKFAST OF CHAMPIONS
ORANGE SLICES CUP COZY

FINISHED MEASUREMENTS
9.5" long x 3" wide

YARN
Knit Picks Shine Sport (60% Pima Cotton, 40% Modal®; 110 yards/50g): MC Grapefruit 25778, CC White 24486; 1 ball each

NEEDLES
US size 4 (3.5mm) needles, or size to obtain gauge
Crochet hook: US size E (3.5mm)

NOTIONS
Two 3/4" buttons
Tapestry needle

GAUGE
24 sts and 30 rows = 4" stockinette stitch

Orange Slices Cup Cozy

Notes:

To decrease the width of the cozy, work fewer repeats of the stitch pattern repeat.

DIRECTIONS
Set Up Rows
Cast on 57 sts in MC using long tail cast on.
Row 1: *K1, P1,* repeat * to * 28 times, K1.
Row 2: *K1, P1,* repeat * to * 28 times, K1.
Row 3: *K1, P1,* repeat * to * 28 times, K1.
Row 4: *K1, P1,* repeat * to * 28 times, K1.
Row 5: Break MC, attach CC. K1, P1, K1, P51, K1, P1, K1.

Body
Work chart 1. Odd (RS) rows are worked from right to left. Even (WS) rows are worked from left to right. Boxed pattern repeat should be worked 8 times per row.

Top Edge
Row 1: Break MC. In CC: K1, P1, K53, P1, K1.
Row 2: Break CC, attach MC. K1, P1, K1, P51, K1, P1, K1.
Row 3: *K1, P1,* repeat * to * 28 times, K1.
Row 4: *K1, P1,* repeat * to * 28 times, K1.
Row 5: *K1, P1,* repeat * to * 28 times, K1.
Row 6: *K1, P1,* repeat * to * 28 times, K1.

Finishing
Bind off all sts. Weave in ends. Block and lay flat to dry. Make crochet loops.

Crochet loops (Make two)
In MC, make slip knot. Using crochet hook, chain nine. Break yarn and pull yarn through last loop to tighten.

Sew buttons onto right edge of cozy. The first button should be placed .5" in from right edge and .5" up from cast on edge. The second button should be placed .5" in from right edge and .5" down from bind off edge. Sew on crochet loops onto left side of cozy. The first loop should be placed .5" up from cast on edge. The second loop should be placed .5" down from bind off edge.

Chart 1

Legend

knit
RS: knit stitch
WS: purl stitch

purl
RS: purl stitch
WS: knit stitch

MC

CC

Pattern repeat

BREAKFAST OF CHAMPIONS
SUNNY SIDE UP PLACEMAT

FINISHED MEASUREMENTS
14" in circumference

YARN
Knit Picks Shine Sport (60% Pima Cotton, 40% Modal®; 110 yards/50g). MC Dandelion 25340, 1 ball; CC White 24486, 2 balls

NEEDLES
US size 4 (3.5mm) DPNs, 16", and 24" circular needles, or size to obtain gauge

NOTIONS
Tapestry Needle
Stitch Markers

GAUGE
24 sts and 30 rows = 4" stockinette stitch

Sunny Side Up Placemat

Notes:

This placemat is worked in the round from the center outward.

Circular Cast On

Pinch the working yarn between the first and middle finger of your left hand so the end of the yarn comes out behind your fingers. Wrap the working yarn tail around the ring and pinky fingers of your left hand, holding the yarn tail firmly with your right hand. Point the tips of these fingers down toward your palm. *Using your right hand, insert the point of your needle (you can use double points or a circular) under the yarn across the back of your ring and pinky fingers (the 'first loop') from front to back. Pass the needle over the working yarn and draw a loop out from under the first loop; this creates one cast-on stitch. YO.* Repeat from * until you have cast on the required number of stitches. Note: If you need an even number of stitches, you will need to cast on the final stitch as a standard yarn over when you begin your first round of knitting. Arrange the stitches on your double point needles to begin knitting in the round. Tug on the yarn tail to draw the stitches into a tighter circle. .

DIRECTIONS

Set Up Rows:

Cast on 8 stitches in MC using size 4 DPNs and a circular cast on. Place marker at the beginning of the round.

Rnd 1: K all sts.

Rnd 2: *K1, YO,* repeat * to * eight times. 16 sts.

Rnd 3: *K1, Ktbl,* repeat * to * eight times.

Body

Rnd 1: *YO, K1,* repeat * to * sixteen times. 32 sts.

Rnd 2: *Ktbl, K1,* repeat * to * sixteen times.

Rnds 3 – 4: K all sts.

Rnd 5: K1, *YO, K1, YO, K3,* repeat * to * seven times, YO, K1, YO, K2. 48sts.

Rnd 6: K1, *Ktbl, K1, Ktbl, K3,* repeat * to * seven times, Ktbl, K1, Ktbl, K2.

Rnds 7 – 8: K all sts.

Rnd 9: K1, *M1, K3, M1, K3,* repeat * to * seven times, M1, K3, M1, K2. 64 sts.

Rnds 10 – 12: K all sts.

Rnd 13: K2, *M1, K3, M1, K5,* repeat * to * seven times, M1, K3, M1, K3. 80 sts.

Rnds 14 -16: K all sts.

Break MC. Attach CC. Work the remaining rnds in CC.

Rnd 17: K2, *M1, K5, M1, K5,* repeat * to * seven times, M1, K5, M1, K3. 96 sts.

Rnds 18 – 20: K all sts.

Rnd 21: K3, *M1, K5, M1, K7,* repeat * to * seven times, M1, K5, M1, K4. 112 sts.

Rnds: 22 – 24: K all sts.

Rnd 25: K3, *M1, K7, M1, K7,* repeat * to * seven times, M1, K7, M1, K4. 128 sts.

Rnds 26 – 28: K all sts.

Rnd 29: K4, *M1, K7, M1, K9,* repeat * to * seven times, M1, K7, M1, K5. 144 sts.

Rnds 30 – 32: K all sts.

Rnd 33: K4, *M1, K9, M1, K9,* repeat * to * seven times, M1, K9, M1, K5. 160 sts.

Rnds 34 – 36: K all sts.

Rnd 37: K5, *M1, K9, M1, K11,* repeat * to * seven times, M1, K9, M1, K6. 176 sts.

Rnds 38 – 40: K all sts.

Rnd 41: K5, *M1, K11, M1, K11,* repeat * to * seven times, M1, K11, M1, K6. 192 sts.

Rnds 42 – 44: K all sts.

Rnd 45: K6, *M1, K11, M1, K13,* repeat * to * seven times, M1, K11, M1, K7. 208 sts.

Rnds 46 – 48: K all sts.

Rnd 49: K6, *M1, K13, M1, K13,* repeat * to * seven times, M1, K13, M1, K7. 224 sts.

Rnd 50: P all sts.

Rnd 51: K all sts.

Rnd 52: P all sts.

Finishing:

Bind off all sts. Weave in ends. Block and lay flat to dry.

Woodsy Kitchen Set

Bring the warm autumn atmosphere of towering trees and their richly colored leaves into your kitchen with the Woodsy Kitchen Set. All three pieces are designed to sit snugly together: the Hand Towel buttons and can hang from your oven or cupboard handle, supporting the Dishcloth and Mug Cozy. This set together creates the look of October trees with texture like bark and deep warm hues. Perfect for you and all your autumn-loving friends, the Woodsy Kitchen Set is quick and easy knitting, great for gift-giving!

Happy Knitting!

Teresa Gregorio

WOODSY
DISHCLOTH

FINISHED MEASUREMENTS
7.5" wide x 10" high

YARN
Knit Picks CotLin (70% Tanguis Cotton, 30% Linen; 123 yards/50g): Pomegranate 24466, 1 ball.

NEEDLES
US 5 (3.75mm) dpns or circular needles, or size to obtain gauge

NOTIONS
Yarn Needle

GAUGE
20 sts and 28 rows = 4" over broken rib pattern, blocked

Dishcloth

Notes:

Beginning with an I-cord "stem", this dishcloth is knit from the top down to form a simple leaf shape. The "stem" loop at the top of allows the Woodsy Dish Cloth to attach to its matching Woodsy Mug Cozy and Woody Hand Towel to make your own leafy tree!

I-cord

Using either DPNs or a circular needle, CO 3 sts. K3 sts. Slide sts to opposite end of the needle and without turning your work, K3 sts. Rep for desired length.

SKKP

Slip one, k2tog, psso.

DIRECTIONS

The dish cloth begins with an I-cord and transitions into a leaf shape.

I-cord

Work an I-cord for 3".

Leaf

Row 1 (RS): Sl 1 kwise, M1, K1, M1, K1. (5 sts)
Row 2 (WS): Sl 1 pwise, K1, P1, K1, P1.
Row 3: Sl 1 kwise, M1, (K1, M1), rep a total of 3 times, K1. (9 sts)
Row 4: Sl 1 pwise, (K1, P1), rep a total of 4 times.
Row 5: Sl 1 kwise, (M1, K1), rep a total of 8 times. (17 sts)
Row 6: Sl 1 pwise, (K1, P1), rep a total of 8 times.
Row 7: Sl 1 kwise, M1, (K1, M1), rep a total of 15 times, K1. (33 sts)
Row 8: Sl 1 pwise, (K1, P1), rep a total of 15 times.
Row 9: Sl 1 kwise, K to end.
Row 10: As Row 8.

Rep Rows 9 and 10 for a total of 7".

Decreasing Leaf

Row 1 (RS): Sl 1 kwise, SKKP, K to last 4 sts, SKKP, K1. (29 sts)
Row 2 (WS): Sl 1 pwise, (K1, P1), rep to end.
Rep Rows 1 and 2 a total of 7 times. There are 5 sts remaining.
Next Row (RS): Sl 1 kwise, SKKP, K1. (3 sts)
Next Row (WS): Sl 1 pwise, K1, P1.
Next Row: SKKP.
Cut yarn, drawing up through last st.

Finishing

Stitch I-cord down to form a loop.
Weave in ends, wash and block to diagram.

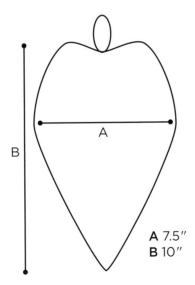

A 7.5"
B 10"

WOODSY
HAND TOWEL

FINISHED MEASUREMENTS
10" wide x 18" high

YARN
Knit Picks CotLin (70% Tanguis Cotton, 30% Linen; 123 yards/50g): Thicket 26995, 1 ball

NEEDLES
US 5 (3.75mm) straight or circular needles, or size to obtain gauge

NOTIONS
Yarn Needle
1" button (ideally a shanked button)

GAUGE
20 sts and 28 rows = 4" over garter stitch, blocked.

Hand Towel

Notes:

This hand towel is designed to hang from any convenient spot in your kitchen. The "branch" at the top folds over to form a loop that secures at the button, and allows the Woodsy Hand Towel to attach to its matching Woodsy Dish Cloth and Woody Mug Cozy to make your own leafy tree!

SKKP

Slip one, k2tog, psso.

DIRECTIONS

The hand towel is knit from the bottom up.

Trunk

CO 49 sts.

Row 1 (RS): Sl 1 kwise, K to end.
Row 2 (WS): Sl 1 pwise, (K5, P1), rep a total of 8 times.
Rep Rows 1 and 2 for 10".

Decreasing Trunk

Row 1 (RS): Sl 1 kwise, (SSK, K1, K2TOG, K1) rep a total of 8 times. (33 sts)
Row 2 (WS): Sl 1 pwise, (K3, P1), rep a total of 8 times.
Row 3: Sl 1 kwise, K to end.
Row 4: Sl 1 pwise, (K3, P1), rep a total of 8 times.

Rep Rows 3 and 4 a total of 3 times.

Next Row (RS): Sl 1 kwise, (SKKP, K1) rep a total of 8 times. (17 sts)
Row 2 (WS): Sl 1 pwise, (K1, P1), rep a total of 8 times.
Row 3: Sl 1 kwise, k to end of row.
Row 4: Sl 1 pwise, (k1, p1), rep a total of 8 times.
Rep Rows 3 and 4 a total of 2 times.

Branch

Row 1 (RS): Sl 1 kwise, K4, SKKP, K1, SKKP, K to end. (13 sts)
Row 2 (WS): Sl 1 pwise, (K1, P1), rep a total of 6 times.
Row 3: Sl 1 kwise, K to end.
Row 4: As Row 2.
Rep Rows 3 and 4 for 5".

Buttonhole

Row 1 (RS): Sl 1 kwise, K3, BO 5, K to end.
Row 2 (WS): Sl 1 pwise, K1, P1, K, CO 5, K1, P1, K1, P1.
Row 3: Sl 1 kwise, SSK, K to 3 sts before end, K2TOG, K1. (11 sts)
Row 4: Sl 1 pwise, (K1, P1), rep a total of 4 times, P2.
Row 5: Sl 1 kwise, SSK, P1, K1, P1, K1, P1, K2TOG, P1. (9 sts)
Row 6: Sl 1 pwise, P1, K1, P1, K1, P1. K1, P2.
Row 7: Sl 1 kwise, SSK, PSSO, BO to last 3 sts, K2TOG, BO remaining st.

Finishing

Stitch button on RS approximately 5" down from buttonhole. Weave in ends, wash and block to diagram.

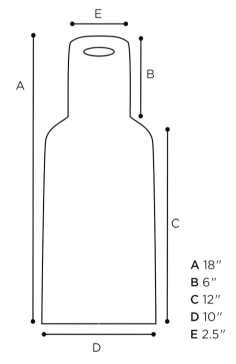

A 18"
B 6"
C 12"
D 10"
E 2.5"

WOODSY
MUG COZY

FINISHED MEASUREMENTS
10" wide x 4.5" high; ties each 9" long

YARN
Knit Picks CotLin (70% Tanguis Cotton, 30% Linen; 123 yards/50g): Clementine 24460, 1 ball

NEEDLES
US 5 (3.75mm) dpn or circular needles, or size to obtain gauge

NOTIONS
Yarn Needle
Waste Yarn

GAUGE
20 sts and 28 rows = 4" over garter stitch, blocked.

Mug Cozy

Notes:

This mug cozy is designed to fit any mug! You can snugly secure the "leaves" that wrap around and drape down your mug with the I-cord ties that extend from the two side leaf tips. The "stem" loop at the top of the cozy allows the Woodsy Mug Cozy to attach to its matching Woodsy Dish Cloth and Woody Hand Towel to make your own leafy tree!

I-cord

Using either dpns or a circular needle, CO 3 sts. K3 sts. Slide sts to opposite end of the needle and without turning your work, K3 sts. Rep for desired length.

SKKP

Slip one, k2tog, psso.

DIRECTIONS

The mug cozy is worked flat from the top down.

Top Edge

CO 9 sts.

Row 1 (RS): Sl 1 kwise, (KFB, K1), rep a total of 4 times.
Row 2 (WS): Sl 1 pwise, (K2, P1), rep a total of 4 times.
Row 3: Sl 1 kwise, (KFB, KFB, K1), rep a total of 4 times. (21 sts)
Row 4: Sl 1 pwise, (K4, P1), rep a total of 4 times.
Row 5: Sl 1 kwise, (KFB, K1, M1, K1, KFB, K1), rep a total of 4 times. (33 sts)
Row 6: Sl 1 pwise, (K7, P1), rep a total of 4 times.
Row 7: Sl 1 kwise, (KFB, K1), rep a total of 16 times. (49 sts)
Row 8: Sl 1 pwise, (K11, P1), rep a total of 4 times.
Row 9: Sl 1 kwise, k to end.
Row 10: Sl 1 pwise, (K11, P1), rep a total of 4 times.

Rep Rows 9 and 10 a total of 3 times.

Right Leaf

Row 1 (RS): Sl 1 kwise, K15, M1, turn. (17 sts), place remaining stitches on waste yarn.
Row 2 (WS): Sl 1 pwise, K3, P1, K to last st, P1.
Row 3: Sl 1 kwise, SSK, K to end. (16 sts)
Row 4: Same as Row 2.

Rep Rows 3 and 4 a total of 8 times. There are now 9 sts on Right Leaf.

Next Row (RS): Sl 1 kwise, SSK, K3, K2TOG, K1. (7 sts)
Row 2 (WS): Sl 1 pwise, K2, P1, K2, P1.
Row 3: Sl 1 kwise, SSK, K1, K2TOG, K1. (5 sts)
Row 4: Sl 1 pwise, K1, P1, K1, P1.
Row 5: Sl 1 kwise, SSKP, K1. (3 sts)
Row 6: Sl 1 pwise, P2TOG, PSSO.
Cut yarn, drawing up through last st.

Center Leaf

Place next 19 sts on needle; remove waste yarn. Attach working yarn with RS facing.
Row 1 (RS): M1, K17, M1, turn. (19 sts)
Row 2 (WS): Sl 1 pwise, K8, P1, K8, P1.
Rows 3, 5, 7, 9, 11, 13 and 15: Sl 1 kwise, SSK, K to last 3 sts, K2TOG, K1. (17 sts)

Row 4: Sl 1 pwise, (K7, P1), rep a total of 2 times.
Row 6: Sl 1 pwise, (K6, P1), rep a total of 2 times.
Row 8: Sl 1 pwise, (K5, P1), rep a total of 2 times.
Row 10: Sl 1 pwise, (K4, P1), rep a total of 2 times.
Row 12: Sl 1 pwise, (K3, P1), rep a total of 2 times.
Row 14: Sl 1 pwise, (K2, P1), rep a total of 2 times.
Row 16: Sl 1 pwise, (K1, P1), rep a total of 2 times.
After Row 16, there are now 5 sts.
Row 17: Sl 1 kwise, SKKP, K1. (3 sts)
Row 18: Sl 1 pwise, P2.
Row 19: SKKP.
Cut yarn, drawing up through last st.

Left Leaf

Place remaining 17sts on needle; remove waste yarn. Attach working yarn with RS facing.
Row 1 (RS): M1, K to end. (17 sts)
Row 2 (WS): Sl 1 pwise, K11, P1, K3, P1.
Rows 3: Sl 1 kwise, K to last 3 sts, K2TOG, K1. (16 sts)
Row 4: Sl 1 pwise, K to last 4 sts, P1, K3, P1.

Rep Rows 3 and 4 a total of 8 times. There are now 9 sts on Left Leaf.

Next Row (RS): Sl 1 kwise, SSK, K3, K2TOG, K1. (7 sts)
Row 2 (WS): Sl 1 pwise, K2, P1, K2, P1.
Row 3: Sl 1 kwise, SSK, K1, K2TOG, K1. (5 sts)
Row 4: Sl 1 pwise, K1, P1, K1, P1.
Row 5: Sl 1 kwise, SSKP, K1. (3 sts)
Row 6: Sl 1 pwise, P2TOG, PSSO.
Cut yarn, drawing up through last st.

Finishing

Make 2 I-cords that are each 9" long. Make 1 I-cord that is 3" long. Stitch each of the 9" I-cord to the tip of the Right and Left leaves. Stitch both ends of the 3" I-cord to the top center of the cozy to form a loop.
Weave in ends, wash and block to diagram.

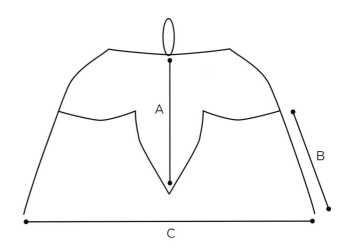

Knots and Loops Kitchen Set

The Knots & Loops Set is a fantastic way to add loads of cozy and complex-looking texture, with the simplest of stitches. A little collection of these coasters would make a fantastic holiday gift. Or play with scale and make them jumbo and use them as placemats or trivets. The dishcloth's unique stitching provides density, making cleaning up a snap. The towel's over-sized loops absorb extra moisture--they're great for drying hands! The washable yarn makes it all a breeze to clean. Enjoy!

Happy Knitting!

Rachel Malis

KNOTS AND LOOPS

WINDOWPANE DISHCLOTH

FINISHED MEASUREMENTS

9.5″ x 8″

YARN

Knit Picks CotLin (70% Tanguis Cotton, 30% Linen; 123 yards/50g): C1 Swan 24134, C2 Moroccan Red 23996, 1 skein each

NEEDLES

US 4 (3.5mm) straight or circular needles, or size to obtain gauge

NOTIONS

Yarn Needle

GAUGE

24 sts and 36 rows = 4″ over Windowpane Stitch Pattern, blocked. Gauge is not critical for this project

Windowpane Dishcloth

Notes:

Pick your two favorite colors. The first will be your "windowpanes" and the second will peek through. The other side, equally pretty, shows the second color more dominantly. Slipping the first stitch of each row will give the project a tidy edge.

Windowpane Stitch Pattern (worked flat)

Row 1: (RS) C1: knit.
Row 2: (WS) C1: knit.
Row 3: C2: k1, sl 1 wyib, *k2, sl 1 wyib; rep from * to last st, k1.
Row 4: C2: k1, sl 1 wyif, *k2, sl 1 wyif; rep from * to last st, k1.

DIRECTIONS

With C1, CO 55 stitches.

Begin working Windowplane Stitch Pattern, slipping the first st of each row.

Rep rows 1-4 for 8" or until desired length.

BO all stitches with C1.

Finishing

Weave in ends. Wash and block to measurements.

KNOTS AND LOOPS
LOOPY TOWEL

FINISHED MEASUREMENTS
12" x18"

YARN
Knit Picks CotLin (70% Tanguis Cotton, 30% Linen; 123 yards/50g): C1 Swan 24134, C2 Clarity 26997, 1 skein each

NEEDLES
US 11 (8.0mm) straight or circular needles, or size to obtain gauge

NOTIONS
Yarn Needle

GAUGE
7.5 stitches and 16 rows = 4" over Loopy Stitch Pattern holding 2 strands togther, blocked. Gauge is not critical for this project

Loopy Towel

Notes:

This stitch produces an oversized terry cloth loop, perfect for drying hands and dishes! Slipping the first stitch of each row creates a nice straight edge.

Loopy Stitch Pattern (worked flat)

Row 1: *K 1 st, but do not allow the stitch to fall off the needle. Bring the working yarn to the front between the two needles. Place your thumb on the working yarn, and wrap the yarn around the top of your thumb, and back between the two needles. Keeping the yarn wrapped around thumb, knit into the same st again. Allow st to fall off the needle, and the loop to fall off your thumb. There are now two new sts and a loop on the right needle. Insert the left needle into the front of the two sts on the right needle, and k together.* Rep between ** across row.
Row 2: Purl.

DIRECTIONS

Holding C1 and C2 together, cast on 30 stitches.

Work Loopy Stitch Pattern, for 18" or desired length, slipping the first st of each row.

BO all sts loosely.

Finishing

Weave in ends. Wash and block to measurements.

KNOTS AND LOOPS
I-CORD COASTER

FINISHED MEASUREMENTS
Approximately 4″ circle

YARN
Knit Picks CotLin (70% Tanguis Cotton, 30% Linen; 123 yards/50g): Moroccan Red 23966. 1 skein

NEEDLES
US 7 (8.0mm) double-pointed or circular needles

NOTIONS
Crochet hook for weaving in ends

GAUGE
36 rows = 4″ in I-cord. Gauge is not critical for this project

I-Cord Coaster

Notes:
Make your i-cord nice and long to give yourself maximum weaving options when you're done!

I-cord
*Knit 1 row. Slide row to other end of needle without turning work. Pull yarn firmly and reapeat from *, creating a tube.

DIRECTIONS
Cast on 4 stitches.

Knit I-cord for 108".

BO all sts, leaving 3" of yarn.

Weave a flat Turk's Head Knot mat with your i-cord. For a helpful video on how to weave a Turk's Head Knot, please see: https://www.youtube.com/watch?v=qFhl09H5mLY

This animation is helpful, too: http://www.animatedknots.com/carrickmat/index.php

It will most likely take several tries to get the shape and size right for your Turk's Head weaving—this is normal! Don't get discouraged!

Finishing
Weave in ends.

ABOUT THE DESIGNERS

Allyson Dykhuizen is a knitwear designer and knitting teacher from Michigan who lives in Chicago. Her patterns have been published in Interweave Knits, Knitscene, and **knit.wear** magazines, by Lion Brand Yarns, and included in the Knit Picks Independent Designer Program. She can be found on Ravelry at sweatshopoflove, self publishes and blogs on her website The Sweatshop of Love, and is editor of Holla Knits.
For pattern support, contact allyson@thesweatshopoflove.com

Faith Schmidt designs under the name DistractedKnits for a very good reason. With nine children in the house, there's always something going on! This has led her to design patterns that are interesting to knit, but are also easy to memorize and "read", in case of one of those all-too-frequent interruptions. Faith can be found online at www.DistractedKnits.weebly.com and on Ravelry, Pinterest, Instagram and Twitter as DistractedKnits.
For pattern support, contact DistractedKnits@hotmail.com

Joyce Fassbender is a biology lecturer in New York City. She recently got a puppy that she's training to be a good knitting dog, but not to knit because, sadly, it can't hold the needles. When not playing with the puppy, she's obsessing over shawls and lace.
For pattern support, contact joycef2@gmail.com

Born in Sault Ste. Marie Ontario, **Beth Major** learned to crochet and knit at a young age from her Grandmother and while the needles confounded her, she really got hooked on crochet. Influenced by her upbringing in Northern Ontario, her designs tend to trend toward items for winter wear and home coziness. With a yarn stash that seems to breed in various closets and corners of her house, she often has at least 4 to 5 projects on the go at any one time and, when an idea sparks inspiration, will happily begin a new crochet project (or projects).
For pattern support, contact crochetgypsy@gmail.com

Teresa Gregorio has been designing knitwear since 2007. Her love of fashion, history, art, knitting and making things happily collide on her blog, Canary Knits. For pattern support, contact: canaryknitsdesigns@gmail.com

Kalurah Hudson's love of the Fiber Arts budded from an early life surrounded by art. But knitting and crocheting has just recently become this Northwest native's newest love. She learned from a friend in late 2008 and now designs her own knit and crochet creations. This happy wife and mom of 3 dreams of some day living on an alpaca farm and starting up a fiber studio with built in coffee bistro. For pattern support, contact kalurah@whiletheyplay.com

Emily Ringelman lives in Baton Rouge, Louisiana, a place known more for alligators and gumbo than its knitting designers, but hey, a passion is a passion. Find her on Ravelry as EmilyRingelman.
For pattern support, contact emily.ringelman@gmail.com

Kendra Nitta's handknits designs have been featured in numerous books and magazines, and are available through Knit Picks and on Ravelry. She also sews and designs quilts. Follow along at www.missknitta.com and @missknitta.
For pattern support, contact missknitta@gmail.com

Rachel Malis's mother and her grandmother Rita taught her how to knit, and re-taught her a couple times, too. You can find her on Etsy at www.etsy.com/shop/RibAndWale or on ribandwale.com.

For pattern support, contact rachel.malis@gmail.com

Abbreviations		M	marker		stitch	TBL	through back loop
BO	bind off	M1	make one stitch	RH	right hand	TFL	through front loop
cn	cable needle	M1L	make one left-leaning	rnd(s)	round(s)	tog	together
CC	contrast color		stitch	RS	right side	W&T	wrap & turn (see
CDD	Centered double dec	M1R	make one right-lean-	Sk	skip		specific instructions
CO	cast on		ing stitch	Sk2p	sl 1, k2tog, pass		in pattern)
cont	continue	MC	main color		slipped stitch over	WE	work even
dec	decrease(es)	P	purl		k2tog: 2 sts dec	WS	wrong side
DPN(s)	double pointed	P2tog	purl 2 sts together	SKP	sl, k, psso: 1 st dec	WYIB	with yarn in back
	needle(s)	PM	place marker	SL	slip	WYIF	with yarn in front
EOR	every other row	PFB	purl into the front and	SM	slip marker	YO	yarn over
inc	increase		back of stitch	SSK	sl, sl, k these 2 sts tog		
K	knit	PSSO	pass slipped stitch	SSP	sl, sl, p these 2 sts tog		
K2tog	knit two sts together		over		tbl		
KFB	knit into the front and	PU	pick up	SSSK	sl, sl, sl, k these 3 sts		
	back of stitch	P-wise	purlwise		tog		
K-wise	knitwise	rep	repeat	St st	stockinette stitch		
LH	left hand	Rev St st	reverse stockinette	sts	stitch(es)		

Knit Picks yarn is both luxe and affordable—a seeming contradiction trounced! But it's not just about the pretty colors; we also care deeply about fiber quality and fair labor practices, leaving you with a gorgeously reliable product you'll turn to time and time again.

THIS COLLECTION FEATURES

Dishie
Worsted Weight
100% Cotton

Comfy Worsted
Worsted Weight
75% Pima Cotton, 25% Acrylic

CotLin
DK Weight
70% Tanguis Cotton,
30% Linen

Shine Sport
Sport Weight
60% Pima Cotton, 40% Modal®

View these beautiful yarns and more at www.KnitPicks.com